Keep Chewing Till It
Stops Kicking

Keep Chewing Till It Stops Kicking

Finding Your Inner Caveman

STEVE GRAHAM

Illustrated by Chris Muir and the Author

CITADEL PRESS
Kensington Publishing Corp.
www.kensingtonbooks.com

CITADEL PRESS BOOKS are published by

Kensington Publishing Corp.
850 Third Avenue
New York, NY 10022

All Kensington titles, imprints, and distributed lines are available at special
quantity discounts for bulk purchases for sales promotions, premiums, fund-
raising, educational, or institutional use. Special book excerpts or customized
printings can also be created to fit specific needs. For details, write or phone the
office of the Kensington special sales manager: Kensington Publishing Corp.,
850 Third Avenue, New York, NY 10022, attn: Special Sales Department;
phone 1-800-221-2647.

CITADEL PRESS and the Citadel logo are Reg. U.S. Pat. & TM Off.

First printing: October 2007

10 9 8 7 6 5 4 3 2 1

Printed in the United States of America

Library of Congress Control Number: 2007933516

ISBN-13: 978-0-8065-2938-7
ISBN-10: 0-8065-2938-5

Contents

FOREWORD

Welcome to my second book, which is actually the third book I've written. If you're here because you bought my first book, *The Good, the Spam, and the Ugly*, I hope you like this one just as much. If you're here because you've been reading my websites over the years, thanks for the continued support. If you like what you see here, check out my next offering, *Eat What You Want and Die Like a Man: The World's Unhealthiest Cookbook*, in 2008. I've been working on it for years, and if you're a big fat glutton like me, you are sure to enjoy it. I also have a website at SteveHGraham.com.

The idea for this book came from my publisher. Senior Editor Gary Goldstein pitched it to me a few months back. Sounded like fun, so here it is. Thanks for the opportunity, dude. And remember, if we get sued by GEICO, I am willing to split the cost of a beach house somewhere in Central America.

Observant readers may note certain questionable factual claims in the pages that follow. For example, you may doubt that early hominids were a favorite snack of tyrannosauruses or that they were routinely eaten by a wily predator known as the giant Jurassic goosefish. It is not necessary to mail me letters taking issue with my controversial assertions. Instead, let me point out that there are publicly funded institutions known as "schools." If you're serious about learning about paleontology, a school might possibly be a better resource than a humor book written by an inebriated fat guy. Just a thought.

If you really want to send me your complaints, go ahead. But remember, they become my intellectual property and you implicitly consent to having them posted on the Internet so that I and my readers can make fun of you.

I want to thank Chris Muir for coming in at the last minute and saving me from the aggravation of doing my own illustrations. If you like his work, go check out his online comic strip Day by Day at www.daybydaycartoon.com. Hopefully his career won't be damaged too much by association with me.

Coral Gables, Florida
July 2007

Introduction
Let's Party Like It's 5 Million B.C.

Last year, I received a peculiar e-mail. A man claiming to be a regular reader of my website said he had made a special discovery of great importance to humanity. He said he had tried to interest the mainstream press in it, but they had blown him off. But because I had written about touchy subjects such as the deplorable lack of pension and insurance benefits in the little-person erotic entertainment industry, he felt that I would be more inclined to have an open mind.

I am not sure he realized I was a humorist. I get that a lot. But having no life, I decided to pursue the matter. And before you know it, he had offered to pay my travel expenses, if I would just fly to Arkansas and hear him out.

Soon I found myself on the tarmac at Hot Springs airport, strolling past the ever-present chickens and pigs as they gleaned discarded french fries and banana peppers from the side of the runway. Inside the terminal, standing as far as possible from the drug-sniffing dogs, I saw an elderly, bespectacled man holding up a cardboard sign reading "Graham." That was my first glimpse of my host, former Cambridge archaeologist Wilfred P. Drambuie-Mason.

In the parking lot, he cleared away the empty pint bottles and Grateful Dead cassettes that filled the passenger seat of his aging Volvo, and he drove me to the nearest Motel 6, where he had already prepared my room. On a card table sat an '80s-vintage slide projector filled with images related to his work. He sat me in a desk chair and began showing slides. At first I was a bit uncomfortable with his terse lecture style, but we both began to loosen up as the drinks he mixed took effect.

DRAMBUIE-MASON:

(clicking projector remote) Do you see?

ME:

Yes.

DRAMBUIE-MASON:

(click) Do you SEE?

ME:

Yes. Say, what's that odd, slightly bitter taste in my frozen margarita? I kind of like it.

DRAMBUIE-MASON:

Nothing to worry about. A little seasoning I picked up during my studies in Oaxaca. *(click)* Do you see?

ME:

How did all these glowing butterflies get in the room?

DRAMBUIE-MASON:

Sorry; I should have warned you about those. They're quite harmless. Unless you provoke them.

ME:

I had no idea butterflies could sing.

DRAMBUIE-MASON:

Blast. I forgot the duct tape. I'll have to keep a careful eye on you.

ME:

I feel fine, Mommy. Let me know when the pancakes are done.

■   ■   ■

The gist of the story is this: While exploring the hills overlooking an agate quarry near the remote town of Chicken Bend, Drambuie-Mason made a startling find. There, on the walls of humble, soot-stained caves, he found primitive art and picture-writing dating back to 5 million B.C.

Using state-of-the-art linguistics software developed by NASA in the search for extraterrestrial life, he managed to translate many of the image series into modern English. The result? A spellbinding narrative of primitive life, in the voice of "Hal," a Miocene era everyman.

Drambuie-Mason's translations overturn one historical preconception after another. They show that early man inhabited central Arkansas long before better-known sites such as Africa's Olduvai Gorge. That more than one race of primitives occupied the area during that time. That creatures thought to have become extinct at the end of the Cretaceous era were in fact alive and well in Arkansas's jungles, rivers, and inland sea.

I shivered as Drambuie-Mason recounted Hal's stories about prehistoric life. Although that may have been my body's reaction to the herbs he put in my drink. I marveled at tales of Hal's encounters with other primitive races with which his kind shared the American heartland. I gaped with wonder at Hal's complaints about dinosaurs using his relatives as throw pillows.

Controversial? Certainly. Likely to be linked by cynics to to Dr. Drambuie-Mason's well-known penchant for cappuccino colonics laced with peyote? Without doubt. But then controversy also followed *Titanic* producer James Cameron when he presented an astounded world with Jesus' swing set. And we all know how that turned out.

At the end of the lecture, or rather, the following Tuesday, when I awoke naked under a nearby overpass, I decided to help Drambuie-Mason by writing this book. It is a collection of items from Hal's diary, expressed in his own voice. In the pages that follow, Hal covers just about every aspect of caveman life, from tool-making to hunting to strategies for not becoming a velociraptor stool.

All that awaits you, and more. But before we begin, a sample— a brief excerpt from Hal's voluminous works—to accustom you to his voice and prepare you for the rude "essays" that lie ahead.

Wednesday, July 9, 5,000,037 B.C.

Man, what a morning. Some days it barely pays to leave the cave.

I got up and walked outside, and right away I realized I'd stepped in something. Tyrannosaurus pie. Up to my waist. Great. Just when you've rolled in all the right stuff and gotten your scent the way you want it, something like this happens. And tyrannosaurus is last year's smell. The guys down by the big communal fire are going to have a ball with this.

Like any rational person, I hooted and beat my chest and flailed my arms. Then I pulled myself out and went to check on the mastodon jerky I set out to dry yesterday. Naturally, it was gone. A whole day of hunting and gathering shot to hell.

I can't stand tyrannosauruses. I wish I could figure out some way to kill the darn things. Unfortunately I have a one-inch forehead and zero capacity for abstract thought.

Maybe my grandkids will come up with something, if there's anything to this "evolution" stuff. The Andersons claim their nephew has no protruding brow ridge. Smug bastards. I think they held him down and beat it in with a rock. Invasive medical procedures to modify your body purely out of vanity seem idiotic and primitive to me. Surely we've made more progress than that.

I decided to go down to the tar pits and see if there was anything worth pulling out and dragging home. And of course, the good stuff—the bison and elk—had already been picked over.

I found one of the neighbors sinking into the goo. Herb Peters. He was pretty upset. I thought about whacking him with my club and making some more jerky, but . . . cannibalism? It's so Oligocene epoch. It's just not hip any more.

I pulled him out, and then we put on the usual aggression displays and went about our business. He just hopped up and down and made barking noises, but I stepped it up a notch by throwing dirt in the air. I think he was impressed.

I better not catch him stealing my material.

I found some pretty berries on the way home. I wondered, should I pick these and feed them to the family? I decided against it. All the other times we've

> **Women. They're good for grooming your back hair and cooking your meat and all. But they're basically two udders in search of a brain.**

eaten these things, a whole bunch of people died. My wife, Susan, thinks there might possibly be some connection.

Women. They're good for grooming your back hair and cooking your meat and all. But they're basically two udders in search of a brain.

I went over to see the chimps, to find out if they had found any good termite mounds to raid. I got nowhere with that. Frankly, they were distant. I know what the problem is. Here we are, standing more or less upright and using language, and well, look at them. Stuck in the past. Running around on all fours like a bunch of creodonts. If they were only a little more open to inter-marriage, crap like this wouldn't happen to them.

And now they feel resentful.

Some of those chimp chicks are hot. And it wouldn't hurt them to marry up to a full biped. But I guess old ways die hard. Chimps are big on tradition. When a chimp comes up with a new way of doing things, do they pull ticks off him and bring him dead lizards and make him feel special? Hell, no. They pull him apart and throw his head in the tar pit. Schmucks.

I could tell my club made them feel inferior. Is that my fault? It's not like I was waving it under their noses. And it's not a status symbol. It's a tool. I mean, yeah, I decorated it with some green stuff that came out of an antelope spleen, and it's probably the most bitchin' tricked-out club within a day's walk, but dang, can't a guy have a little style? What am I? Amish?

I swear, chimps have absolutely no game. I don't mean to sound like a racist or anything.

Long story short, I ended up bringing home bear dung again. And of course, I caught hell from Susan. She's always putting me down because no one in her family has opposable big toes. She thinks I'm too stupid to be a good provider because my forebrain is so small. Always with the size jokes. Great way to build my confidence when I'm psyching myself up for a mastodon hunt or something.

I told her it's not like I'm a monkey or anything. I'm not like my grandpa, who ate with one foot while using the other to pick his nose. With effort, I can pick up and manipulate small objects. Big

I'm not like my grandpa, who ate with one foot while using the other to pick his nose.

deal. She's not perfect. Her mom has posture like a gorilla. If she doesn't watch it she gets calluses on her nipples.

The kids got on my back, too. Literally. I brushed them off with my club and told them there were chimp kids who would give anything for a handful of fresh bear dung full of undigested blueberries. It's loaded with antioxidants. But you know how kids are these days. If it isn't mastodon or bison, they turn up their noses at it, which is saying a lot, considering the way their noses look to start with.

I fear for the next generation. When I was a kid and my dad brought home dung, I took it and thanked him for it and called him "sir," or a guttural noise to that effect. These kids today, they have no idea what it's like to grow up in the tail end of an ice age and have to work for a living. Spoiled punks. Back in my dad's day, they would never have gotten away with it. My brother Manny had an attitude like that. And guess what happened to him? Jerky. That's what old-time dads were like.

I miss Dad. I still use his femur to open Brazil nuts.

Keep Chewing Till It
Stops Kicking

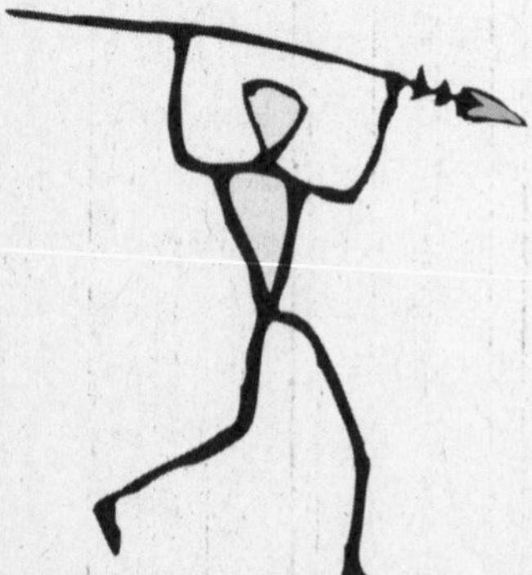

Housing
Uh, *Hello?*—"*Cave*" Men

I thought future generations might want to know what our lives are like, now that we have all this great technology. I figured I'd scrape it out on the walls of my cave in simple pictures even a *Homo habilis* could understand. It's important to preserve knowledge, because we could lose all this stuff, and then where would our great-grandchildren be? For example, instead of modern inventions like the little stick, the big stick, and the great big stick, they'd only have the stick.

The stick was great in its time—don't get me wrong. Sometimes size isn't critical, like when you're throwing a stick on a fire. Other times, size is everything. Like in our space program.

For years now we've been throwing sticks up in the air, hoping one would keep going and hit one of the lights in the sky. To punish it for being higher than us. So far, we haven't had a completely successful mission. But the results get better and better, and they all point in one direction. Smaller sticks.

Seems like we make an important jump in stick technology in almost every generation. In my grandfather's time it was "Before you use the stick, take it off the tree."

That was very big. Before that, we generally hit our food with branches that were still connected. If the food wasn't standing right next to the tree, you went hungry. I can't tell you how many guys starved to death under a tree, waiting for a mimetodon to walk by.

So anyway, I thought I'd record some of this stuff so that future generations would have lives like ours, full of luxury and progress and dignity.

Hang on. I have to lie on my face and pretend to be a heap of dung. Tyrannosaurus . . .

He's gone now.

The basic housing unit these days is the cave. The latest thing in non-detached multi-family dwellings. The cave has made a huge difference in our lives. Before the cave, we just stood around outside, hoping it wouldn't rain too much and that lightning wouldn't strike.

> **The cave has made a huge difference in our lives. Before the cave, we just stood around outside, hoping it wouldn't rain too much and that lightning wouldn't strike.**

We worked on ways to deal with lightning. My uncle figured lightning only hit people who were scared of it, so he developed a strategy. You get a really, really long spear, and when there's a thunderstorm, you go stand on a hill and you raise the spear as high as you can and you threaten the lightning with it.

Unfortunately he died. Nine seconds into the first test. We aren't positive what the answer is. Current consensus? Longer spear.

It's not like we didn't have caves in the past. I mean, they were always there. We didn't carve them or anything. But we didn't go inside much. We had found that stuff burns better in caves because rain and snow can't get to it, so that's where we put our fires. With all the smoke, you really couldn't go in and hang around. So we stood outside and ran in once in a while, just long enough to do a few turns and feel the heat. Or we'd put meat on the fire, run out, run in, turn it, run out, run in, turn it again, and so on.

Eventually we realized we could keep a big communal fire going under a big centrally located ledge and run get some burning wood whenever our household fires went out. So we shoveled the ashes out of our caves and moved in.

While he was getting some fermented berry juice to celebrate, his kids plopped on the bear and sat facing a drawing on the opposite wall.

That same week, we invented the couch.

The first couch was actually a dead bear. A guy killed it for food and dragged it inside for his wife to butcher, and while he was getting some fermented berry juice to celebrate, his kids plopped on the bear and sat facing a drawing on the opposite wall.

Right away, everyone knew this was a major discovery

Pretty soon everyone wanted a dead bear to sit on, and some people were adding a couple of dead antelope to create little seating areas. The problems with this plan became obvious after a few days of warm weather. After that, we emptied the skins and stuffed them with dry grass. And of course dung.

I can't say enough about dung. Building material, medication, artistic medium, hair dressing, condiment . . . dung does it all.

I can't say enough about dung. Building material, medication, artistic medium, hair dressing, condiment . . . dung does it all. I used it as pigment for the paint you're seeing right now. Except—and I can't really explain this—the paint I use to draw dung. For some reason, I get better results with mulberry juice.

Getting a good bear couch is a lot of aggravation, but smaller items of furniture are easier to come by. For example, little leather cushions are really common. Thanks to our spectacular infant mortality rate. And the skulls make great bowls.

Once you have your seating area set up, it's nice to get a big flat rock and put it in front of the couch, to put your feet on. Then you can sit there scratching yourself and eating nuts and hollering for your wife to bring you berry juice. If she's smaller than you.

Me, I get up and get my own berry juice.

Before we started using flat rocks for tables, we used to make our kids get on their hands and knees and put our feet on their backs. But they always collapsed after a few hours. And you couldn't set anything hot on them.

The sleeping area is generally a big scooped-out place in the floor of the cave, covered with skins. And padded generously. With dung.

Caves come in a number of types.

1. *The Ranch Cave.* This is a cave with one or two mouths pretty much at ground level, with two to four sleeping areas.

2. *The Cave Condo.* These are small caves in the side of a cliff, and people on the higher levels have to use vines to get in and out. Economical, but not a great choice if you sleepwalk.

3. *The Burrow.* Cheap and convenient, and you can dig it yourself. And animals fall in, so you don't have to hunt so much. But you pay a price during the rainy season. Or when a dinosaur steps in it.

Burrows have become a lot more popular since the start of the Cave Bubble. It used to be that caves were reasonably priced, or you just killed whoever already lived in them. Then we developed the concept of real estate speculation, and suddenly the price of a cave went from a couple of dead elk to, say, three bison. And some people now buy several caves and leave them empty while the price goes up. Or they sweep out the bones and antlers, smoke out the bats, spruce the sleep areas up—with nicer dung—and do a "cave flip."

This works so well sometimes they can sell the cave back to the same people they bought it from. And they have no idea it's the same cave. In fact, neither do the sellers. Memory takes up space, and most of us have heads only slightly larger than our fists.

We have a group that does something really cool, called Extreme Cave Makeover. They find a family that's down on its luck, and they have them move out of their rundown cave for a while, and they fix it up real nice.

Then they keep it.

Division of authority in a cave works like this. The woman is in charge of everything inside the cave, from the mouth back. The man is in charge of the little area outside the mouth, where the fire is. The barbecue area.

It's always been this way. I say it's because men are naturally gifted cooks. Susan says it's because only men are stupid enough to stand outside, where predators can see them, and risk falling into a big roaring fire. Because what are you if a tyrannosaurus sees you fall in the fire? A hot hors d'oeuvre.

I have some special rocks and logs arranged around the fire pit, where my buddies and I can lounge around and drink berry juice while the meat cooks. Susan used to come out and try to rearrange the furniture or decorate the place with skins and seashells. For some reason that made me really really mad. So she quit. Now we have an understanding. She doesn't mess with my barbecue area, and I don't use her decorative seashells for club practice.

If you're shopping for a cave, I can give you a little advice.

- Before you buy, have your cave inspected. Last winter my cousin got a great price on a cave. Seemed like a real bargain. Then spring came. And woke up the snakes.

- Try to find a cave with at least two mouths. Then when a predator runs in one mouth, you can run out the other. This also works for in-laws. Alternative: Stay farther in the cave than your slowest child.

- When looking for a cave by the ocean, never shop at low tide.

Caves aren't perfect. For one thing, because one end is always open, people and animals can pretty much enter at will.

Once I started to have an idea how to fix this. I thought maybe

I could take a few logs and make them into a big flat thing and fix them so that they somehow blocked the door of the cave but could be moved easily when I wanted to go in or out. But instead of working out the details I decided to rub blue clay in my hair and jump up and down while hooting for no apparent reason. By the time it was over, I had forgotten all about my invention.

One of our neighbors had an idea. He went in his cave and had some friends roll a huge rock over the opening. It seems to work real well. That was two years ago, and in all that time, nobody has managed to break in.

Or out.

It's impossible to keep animals out if they're not scared of the fire outside the cave. That's why I always encourage the neighbors' kids to play at our house. That way when a velociraptor wanders in, I have something I can toss him without upsetting Susan. When the neighbors come looking for their kid, I say he went for a walk by the tar pit.

A lot of people are into fixing up their caves. We have a guy who makes a living telling people how to do it. His name is Bob, and he has a seminar kind of a thing he calls *This Old Cave*. People go down and sit in a circle and give him stuff, and he gives them advice. He has a pal named Norm who helps out. It goes like this:

Bob:

Today on *This Old Cave*, we're going to start with some great advice about shoring up weak places in your ceiling. Norm here is an expert carpenter, so he's going to tell you what to use. Norm?

Norm:

I'd have to go with a stick, Bob.

BOB:

Great, Norm. Moving on, are you tired of throwing your meat on the ground to dry? We can help you with that. We have a great device that holds the meat up until it's ready to take down and hide from the neighbors. Norm?

NORM:

Three sticks, Bob. Tied at the top with an antelope tendon.

BOB:

Good job, Norm. Finally, we're going to show you how to construct a crude platform to keep your bottom off the cold cave floor. Take it away, Norm.

NORM:

Bunch of sticks. Laid out side by side.

BOB:

Wow, sticks are really something.

NORM:

Yes they are, Bob. Sticks are quite amazing.

BOB:

By the way, today's seminar is sponsored by Bob and Norm's Stick Emporium.

■ ■ ■

I don't know if we'll always live in caves. Once, a guy tried building a freestanding shelter out of rocks and mud. He stacked the rocks in kind of a box shape and used the mud to hold it together, and when it dried, it was pretty sweet. You could make this thing any size you wanted, and you could lay it out however you liked.

People got really envious when they saw this thing, and they went out and gathered rocks and mud—or they bought materials at Bob and Norm's new Mud and Rock Factory Outlet, also known as Cave Depot. And they started to build their own shelters. Then a brachiosaurus noticed the first guy's shelter and saw the sharp corners on the roof and tried to use one to scratch its behind. After the place collapsed, he turned around and marked his territory on it—to the tune of about seven hundred gallons. That kind of put a damper on the construction craze. Luckily, Bob and Norm's return policy was "store credit only."

> **We had a real problem with people who couldn't afford to live in caves. We called them "the caveless."**

We had a famine and firewood shortage a while back (more on that later), and during that time, we had a real problem with people who couldn't afford to live in caves. We called them "the caveless."

They claimed they were regular, decent people who were just down on their luck, and I guess some of them were, but an awful lot of them spent their time lying on the ground drinking fermented berry juice. And they smelled even worse than the rest of us.

They used to sit by the path, yelling "WILL WORK FOR FOOD." However, if you offered one a job, he would look really surprised and say he would love to talk to you, but he had to go to the latrine cliff. Which was not very convincing because they

generally just did their business on the path. And if you gave
them food, they traded it for more berry juice.

On our feast days, it became fashionable to go and feed the
caveless before having our own dinners. So people would drag
their kids down to the communal fire and dole out pterodactyl
breast and mashed tubers for an hour or two. And it made them
feel all warm and fuzzy because this was the only time they and
the caveless actually made eye contact.

But eventually the caveless started complaining about the food
and the service, and not long after that, instead of waiting to be
fed, they formed gangs and went into people's caves and took
their food by force. And once they had been in your cave, the
smell was permanent.

We finally realized we had to do something. But a police action
was out of the question, because the police refused to touch them.
Then we had a great idea. We told them we were having a party
for them, and we rounded them up by the communal fire and
gave them all the free berry juice they could drink. And when
they were all unconscious, we poured wildebeest blood all over
them, went indoors, and waited for a tyrannosaurus to pick up
the scent.

What we didn't realize was that their preexisting smell was so
bad, no tyrannosaurus would go near them.

Fortunately, hyenas are not so persnickety.

Caveless advocates gave us a hard time for that, but even they
admit cavelessness is not nearly the problem it used to be.

2

Food

Keep Chewing Till It Stops Kicking

Food is pretty easy to come by at this point in history. We have learned an important fact, to wit: just about anything that moves contains meat. This has resulted in greatly improved food gathering since people no longer waste their time looking for meat inside rocks and trees.

We eventually drew the obvious conclusion: Cannibalism reduces fertility.

We had some problems when folks realized that the "If it moves, it's meat" rule applied to human beings. Who were readily available and not hard to sneak up on. For a while, hunting was really easy and productive, but in time we noticed that in spite of how great we were doing, our population was mysteriously dropping. We eventually drew the obvious conclusion: Cannibalism reduces fertility. Now we try not to overdo it.

Big animals are always tempting. Kill a gopher and you get bites all over your hands and a small snack that poops out and leaves you hungry before sundown. Kill a bear and you have meat for weeks. Plus street cred. On the other hand, the bear knows that if it eats you and your family, it gets a fine meal and a free cave. It's too bad we're not bright enough to grasp concepts like risk management and cost efficiency.

We used to eat everything raw, but then we discovered fire, and since then, cooked food has been very big. In the early days of fire, most cooked meat was eaten rare—because we were holding it over the fire with our bare hands. We moved on to medium and well-done after we discovered the spit.

Okay, that's not quite true. We moved on after we discovered you could secure meat on a spit by running it through, instead of holding it on. With your bare hands.

We have a few seasonings we like a lot. We get salt from the ocean, and then there's clay, and of course, dung.

We're trying to improve our cuisine. There's a guy who teaches people how to cook. People gather around and watch, and it goes like this:

FOOD GUY:
(cooking a wildebeest on open fire) Should I kick it up a notch?

AUDIENCE:
(hooting, chest-pounding, beating of foreheads against rocks)

FOOD GUY:
(Walks over to an audience member and BAM! hits him with club, throws him on fire.)

■   ■   ■

He has a product he sells. He calls it "Essence of Food Guy." I'm pretty sure it's mostly dung.

Let me tell you about a few of our favorite eating animals.

1. Tyrannosaurus

Wouldn't you know it? The hardest one to catch is the one that tastes best. The meat is tender and juicy, and the fat makes an excellent beverage.

Tyrannosaurus meat is costly due to the way we capture them. I'll tell you how it works. First, ten guys get together and draw straws. Then whoever gets the short straw runs out in front of a tyrannosaurus and yells "BOO!" After it eats him, we

Dung isn't just a seasoning. You can also eat it as a main dish. The key to getting good dung is to get far away from the village so that you're sure it's not people dung. Because that would be disgusting.

repeat the process. Until it eats so much it gets sleepy. Then, when it curls up for a nap, whoever is still alive and has the shortest remaining straw goes out and hits it in the head with an axe.

Generally, it eats him, too. So we send another guy. Sooner or later, we win. When you're hunting tyrannosauruses, perseverance is the key. You have to stay the tyrannosaurus course.

I'll tell you what I hate. When, say, guy number five is sliding down the tyrannosaurus's throat, and guy number six starts yelling "QUAGMIRE!" Fortunately, it doesn't ruin the hunt. Because the noise gets him noticed by the tyrannosaurus. After that, guy number seven generally behaves pretty well.

Here's another tip: It pays to hunt with stupid guys. So far, I've been on twelve hunts, and every time I've been guy num-

Mastodons are front-heavy, so by the time you find one, sometimes all that's showing above the tar is the crotch.

ber ten. That's because I always volunteer to draw my straw first. If I hunted with smart guys, the guy with the straws would realize he should cover them up so that you couldn't see how long they were. Instead of throwing them on the ground and shouting, "Good luck, everybody!"

2. Mammoths/Mastodons

I include mammoths and mastodons in the same category because I have no idea what the difference between them is. They're big. They have long noses. They smell. Like we say here in the village, "Six of one, nine of the other."

Killing a mastodon is no easy task, even for a strapping four-foot hominid with seven-inch biceps. If you aggravate one, instead of being intimidated, it may just grab you and use you to clean its ears.

The easist way to get mastodon meat is to wait until one falls in the tar pit and dies. The problem with this is that mastodons are front-heavy, so by the time you find one, sometimes

> **Most mastodon is eaten raw. But it's great cooked. I like to roast some tubers and roll them up in a toasted ear. Makes a nice wrap.**

all that's showing above the tar is the crotch. It pays to do your shopping early. And be sure you don't fall off the mastodon, because around here, anything stuck in the tar legally becomes food.

That's not a hundred percent true. We have a law called the Five-Second Rule. If you can pull yourself out of the tar in five seconds or less, you're not food. However, your neighbors are allowed to throw you back in.

Because of the way we get it, most mastodon is eaten raw. But it's great cooked. I like to roast some tubers and roll them up in a toasted ear. Makes a nice wrap.

3. Brontosauruses

This is a long dinosaur that's big in the middle and small at both ends. They don't eat meat, so it's safe to walk right up to them. What you do is, you approach from the front, holding some greens or some fruit, and when the brontosaurus brings its head closer to investigate, *POW!* you knock its brains out.

I cannot overstress the importance of hitting the right end. If you hit the tail by mistake, the brontosaurus will crack it like a whip and flick you halfway across Pangaea.

The new name for brontosauruses is apatosaurus. I usually get it wrong. It's hard to remember. It's easier to remember the old name, because it means "thunder lizard," and brontosaurus gives me gas.

4. Chimpanzee

I know it's rude to eat your neighbors, but it's hard to resist because these guys are so stupid. You show one something shiny, and he walks up and stares at it, and *POW!* your buddy nails him from behind with the club.

The club guy has to be really quiet, though, because chimps are very strong, and they're insecure about their intelligence. They hate it when they realize you're messing with them or in any way condescending. When that happens, you still do okay, because you and the chimp split the club guy's remains. And if it's a girl chimp, maybe you get lucky. In fact, you can pretty much count on it. Even if you try to run away.

It happens with guy chimps, too, only I wouldn't call that "getting lucky." Much the opposite.

It's not cheating. Cheating is when you get busy with another person. Having a fling with a chimp is no worse than having a fling with a prairie dog or a wild pig. Or a nice ripe papaya.

Maybe this isn't the place to discuss my hobbies.

5. Mesohippus

This is a grazing animal that has a long face, hooves, and a mane. Hard to catch, but the meat is excellent.

One time, a guy saw mesohippuses running around in a field and he had an idea. You put a bunch of these things together and turn them loose and let them run from one place to another, and you bet on which one gets there first. It sounded like fun, so we tried it. Unfortunately, they all ran in different directions.

Then he had another idea. We should get guys to sit on their backs and make the mesohippuses go where we wanted. So we rounded them up again and gave it a shot. But it turns out they don't pay much attention to verbal commands. You'd be on his back yelling, "TWICE AROUND THE TAR PIT, HORSIE!" and he would run to a tree with a low-hanging branch and scrape you off. And once you're on the ground, they bite you.

Finally, we got it right. We have ten or twelve guys race, and each one carries a mesohippus. The races are short, and they don't run too fast, but at least they all end up in the same place. The mesohippuses don't seem to mind. Although they look confused.

It's funny; the athletes always lose when they bet on someone else. I guess betting against yourself is bad luck.

This happens so often, they're thinking of banning betting against yourself down at Bob and Norm's Off-Track Wagering Parlor.

6. Clams

With clams, you just go down to the water and dig them out or pick them up.

The big drawback to clam hunting is the giant Jurassic goosefish. This is an enormous, sharp-toothed, murderous fish that hunts by lying on the bottom of the ocean, wiggling its tongue. Which, on the end of it, has a lure. Resembling a clam.

> Clams are wonderful. They taste great, they can't run away, and we even use their shells as currency.

There are some subtle clues that it isn't a real clam. Like the pair of giant, gaping nostrils several feet behind it. Also, there is a simple test. Grab the clam. If a goosefish eats you, it was fake.

Goosefishes really like human flesh. And since they're developing lungs and legs these days, if one misses you on the first snap, it can get up and chase you back to your cave.

In fact, sometimes when you get up in the morning, they're outside. Waiting.

7. Pterodactyl

Pterodactyl meat is very popular. We used to eat mostly breast meat and drumsticks. But then Bob and Norm found out people would pay ridiculous prices for seasoned pterodactyl wings. So they opened Bob and Norm's Pangaea Fried Pterodactyl. It was the first store in the village to have a walk-through.

Once a year, we have a holiday where every family roasts a pterodactyl. We stuff it with grain and surround it with roasted tubers, and we sit around it at the wheel and thank the Big Ball of Light in the Sky for things like health, prosperity, dung, and opposable thumbs.

Seems like every family has one member who gets drunk on berry juice and starts feeling sorry for himself and picking fights and ruining the holiday for everyone. When you're trying to decide who should go get clams to put in the stuffing, this person is a great choice.

We also eat a lot of fruits, vegetables, and nuts. They're not nearly as interesting as animals. You just walk up to them and grab them. Some guys try to make it more of an event than it really is. But you look fairly stupid sneaking up on a melon with a spear in your hand.

3

Tools

And I Don't Just Mean the In-Laws

Life is pretty easy, now that we've developed a wide array of sweet tools. I'll give you a list.

1. The Rock

This was the first tool. The credit for inventing it goes to a *Homo erectus* named Murray.

One day Murray and his brother Earl were hunting lizards. It works like this. You reach into a crack between two rocks and feel around, and if you feel a lizard, you pull it out and throw it to your buddy, and he puts it in the bag with the others. The problem with this is that snakes like cracks, too. And so do giant scorpions.

Murray was tired of scorpion stings, and he wished he could stick his head in the cracks and see what was in there. But his head wouldn't fit. Then he remembered something that happened a week earlier in his village. A guy was standing around under a cliff, and a huge boulder rolled down and landed on him. When they rolled it off, he was wide and thin and flat. And for a while, his family used him as an area rug.

Murray gave Earl a big rock and got down on the ground and told him to hit him in the head with it.

The procedure was a qualified success and a huge technological advance. But Earl caught hell from Murray's widow.

A year later, a guy survived the procedure and recovered well enough to go lizard hunting. Then he died. From snakebites to the face.

Since then, we've come up with all sorts of variations on the rock. The round rock. The flat rock. The pointy rock. The wooden rock. And my favorite: the suggestively shaped party rock.

Hammer rocks, throwing rocks, anvil rocks, table rocks, chair rocks . . . the variety is endless. And rocks form the basis for the next generation of tools.

2. Stone Tools

The first stone tool was the knife. A guy dropped a rock, and it broke in half, and he found that the sharp edge was good for cutting things. First thing you know, his wife was cutting animals in pieces before cooking them. Before that, you cooked the whole animal all at once. When you were hungry, you had to walk over and gnaw on it.

The second stone tool was the spearhead. It's basically a really pointy stone knife, and you can use it as a projectile to kill game or get guests out of your cave after a long party.

The main problem with early spearheads was, we still hadn't discovered the fully detached stick. We had nothing to attach the spearhead to, so instead of a spearhead, it was more like . . . a head. If you wanted to kill a mammoth, you had to run up to him, hold the spearhead against him, and push. And while you were doing that, he would usually wrap his trunk around one of your ankles and use you as a flyswatter.

If you wanted to kill a mammoth, you had to run up to him, hold the spearhead against him, and push.

3. The Ax

After the spearhead, we developed the ax. This is a heavy rock that's sharp on one side. Works a lot better on the end of a stick. With an ax, you can cut legs off dead animals, take limbs off of trees, and turn your enemies' skulls into attractive nut dishes.

Our local doctor, Dr. Ed, has a million uses for his ax. He uses it mainly for removing splinters.

Also useful during fee disputes.

4. The Stick

I mentioned this earlier. It's just a piece of a tree. Depending on the size, you can use it for a number of jobs. Small sticks are good for starting fires and cleaning your ears. Medium sticks are good for prying things and whacking small game, and they make nice tool handles. Long, thin sticks are good for spears. Big sticks make great clubs.

The club is such a great killing tool, we actually had a campaign to ban it. On the one side, there were people who thought everyone had the right to keep and bear clubs. On the other, there was the Coalition to Stop Club Violence.

The Coalition was composed mainly of unusually hairy single women who refused to eat animals. But it also attracted a number of really big guys who had figured out how sweet life would be if their smaller neighbors didn't have clubs.

> **Some guys formed the National Club Association. Their leader was an old guy named Charlie. He once held up his club and hollered, "I'll give up my club when they pry it out of my cold, dead feet."**

In response, some guys formed the National Club Association. Their leader was an old guy named Charlie. He once held up his club and hollered, "I'll give up my club when they pry it out of my cold, dead feet."

That was inspiring. Ironically, he died the next day.

The Coalition managed to get a ban passed at a High Council meeting. After that, life was supposed to be peaceful and idyllic. However, people spotted the obvious loophole and started jabbing each other with spears. Then we banned spears. Then they started hitting each other with rocks. So we banned rocks.

Pretty soon, we were down to one approved tool. The small blunt twig. Coincidentally, that's when the firewood shortage and famine began.

Fortunately, the ban had a sunset provision. They called it a sunset provision because it went into effect on a certain day at sunset. That night the High Council had an emergency meeting to consider extending the ban, and the NCA guys showed up and brought the Coalition people with them. In a series of small leather pouches.

Since then club laws have been pretty relaxed.

5. Fire

Fire isn't exactly a tool, but it might as well be, because it makes life a hell of a lot easier. We cook with it, it keeps us warm, it's useful for medical treatment, and when we get bored, we throw stuff in it to see if anything cool happens.

I can't say fire was invented. It was always here. Usually right after lightning strikes. We just grabbed it and took it home.

We didn't always have a communal fire to rely on when the fires by our caves went out. One time, we ran out of fire and we had to wait three weeks until the next thunderstorm. Even then, the lightning didn't seem to want to hit any trees. Fortunately, my wife's uncle was tired of raw meat, so he went outside to call the sky filthy names, and by a stroke of luck, lightning hit him and set his hair on fire. Then, of course, we faced an ethical dilemma. Put it out or hold his head up to a bundle of dry twigs.

You can't say we weren't fair. He got to vote just like everybody else.

The sad thing is, five minutes later, lightning hit a big dry tree trunk ten feet away.

Hey. We had no way of knowing that was going to happen.

6. The Wheel

This one is really fantastic. A few years back, somebody figured out that you could make big rocks a lot more useful by

modifying them. So he got an ax and a big rock, and he started
hammering and chipping. And he made the rock round and flat,
with a big hole in the middle. That was the first wheel.

After that, when people went to his house for dinner, they sat
around the wheel, ate roast mastodon, and shoved the bones
down the hole. It was brilliant.

Obviously, that's not the only use for the wheel. Little ones
make wonderful earrings and navel decorations.

A few years back, some guy made four wheels and ran sticks
through the centers and put them at the corners of a big wooden
platform. Then he put his family on the platform and pushed
them through the village while the wheels turned.

I honestly think that was the dumbest invention I've ever seen.
Well . . . second-dumbest. After the tyrannosaurus caller.

Wheels that big take a long time to make, and here this guy
was, wasting four of them. And for some reason, all the women
in the village wanted to ride on his invention and mate with him.
You'd wonder where your wife was, and you'd find her lying on
the back of this thing alone, with her knees up in the air. They
said it just felt natural.

The High Council passed a law saying wheels could only be
used for important things like tables and jewelry and sex toys.
The inventor argued that because of the way his invention
affected women, it *was* a sex toy. So they fined him three antelope for contempt of council. Their fancy way of calling him a
wise guy.

That thing caused a lot of trouble, so a bunch of us got
together and rolled it into the tar pit. We were afraid frivolous
doodads like that would distract inventors from creating things
that were actually useful. Like dung alternatives. Imagine an
unlimited supply of synthetic dung.

That wasn't the end of the wheel story. A guy who made

wheels for a living noticed that if you let go of them while you were working on them, they had a tendency to roll and get away from you. That was really aggravating and also dangerous, especially if your workshop was uphill from the place where your kids liked to play. He discovered that wheels were a lot more stable if you flattened one side.

That put an end to the rolling problem.

Now we have wheels all over the place. Big wheels. Little wheels. Wood wheels. Stone wheels. They're just fantastically useful.

If only we had an easy way to transport them.

4

Clothing
Sometimes Back Hair Just Isn't Enough

It may come as a surprise to you that we wear clothing. We've been doing it for several generations. I think it started when our body hair thinned out to the point where you could see a lot of parts that had previously been possible to detect only by feel.

It was pretty bad, I hear. You'd be down by the communal fire trying to enjoy your part of an apatosaurus rib, and you'd look over and some guy would be standing with one leg up on a log and *whoa*, there went your appetite. Check, please. I'll take my rib to go.

One benefit to the hair thing was that as it got thinner, it got easier to tell chicks from dudes. Before all that stuff came into view, there were a lot of married couples who went years not realizing they were the same sex. You can imagine how stupid a guy feels when he learns his wife is male. You think things like "No wonder she never nagged."

> **You can imagine how stupid a guy feels when he learns his wife is male. You think things like "No wonder she never nagged."**

**Some guy would be standing with one leg up
on a log and <u>whoa</u>, there went your appetite.**

You would think adding clothing would make it harder to tell
the sexes apart, but you would be wrong. It made it tons easier.
Not only did women dress different; they took hours to do it. No
one knows why. Men would be out of the cave right after sunrise,
hunting and gathering and schmoozing, and it would be noon
before women came out to criticize.

It got even worse when women invented makeup. They found
that by smearing mud and beeswax and fruit juice on their faces,
they could make themselves considerably less terrifying. Makeup
added another hour to their routines. And for some reason they
blamed it on men.

The scary thing about makeup is that it works pretty good on
men, too. Go to a dance, overdo the berry juice, spend two hours
grunting up a hot girl with amazingly red lips, and you may
wake up in the morning next to a guy. And you may feel really
disgusted with yourself for sleeping with him. After doing it for
a week or two.

I can give you a basic rundown of the things we typically wear. First, the men.

1. *The Bearskin Housedress.* This is a fetching little number. You kill a bear, and then you get the skin off and dry it, and you fix it so you have a skirty sort of thing around your lower body, held up by a strappy sort of part over one shoulder. It's cool and comfortable and not likely to fall off while you're running from predators. You can still gross out diners down by the communal fire, but you have to get that leg up pretty high.

2. *The Bearskin Miniskirt.* Sort of like the housedress, only no strap. It only goes up to your waist. You hold it up by tying a vine around you. It's lighter and cooler than the housedress, but it's much less secure when you have a tyrannosaurus chasing you. It's hard to run fast with one of these things around your ankles. Although you can probably shuffle faster than you think, with a tyrannosaurus breathing down your neck.

The skin doesn't absolutely have to be bear. It can be giant sloth or bison or mammoth. Just about anything. Even dinosaur. That's actually a good idea, because on mammals, the cheaper pieces of leather tend to have nipples. Or worse.

Here's a tip: To avoid defeating the whole purpose of clothes, cross those legs at the ankle, not the knee. Primitive meals are disgusting enough without your help.

I don't know if there is any point in talking about women's fashion. It's pretty much the same stuff, only

"Tell me you're not leaving the cave dressed like that."

for some reason everything is a lot shorter. And again, they blame men for this. Even when we say things like "Tell me you're not leaving the cave dressed like that."

Some women wear brassieres fashioned from vines or leather strips attached to round containers such as coconut halves. This is a little hard to figure out. Brassieres give the bosom an off-putting round, firm, smooth look. Not nearly as tantalizing as long, flat, hairy, wrinkled, and more or less triangular. Oh, man. I get excited just writing about it. Hold on while I go outside and beat my chest for a minute. . . .

I'm back.

We're not big on hats. One guy I knew tried to make a hat out of an empty dinosaur egg, to keep the sun off him. It worked fine until he laid down for a nap. And a triceratops sat on his head.

Sometimes important guys wear hats. Like Dr. Ed, the shaman. He made a hat out of a bear's head, with the nose and everything still on it, and fur hanging down the back, and paws hanging over his shoulders. It can be really intimidating when he asks you medical questions with that bear glaring at you from the top of his head.

If you have a hat like that, don't wear it outdoors when the bears are mating. Dr. Ed learned that lesson the hard way.

Jewelry is popular. Necklaces, especially. They're great for men, because you can use them to advertise what an amazing guy you are. For example, you kill a bear or a tyrannosaurus and you make a necklace out of the claws and teeth.

The most likely way to hurt a giant dinosaur is to become a fatal bowel obstruction.

Chicks will wear out a guy wearing tyrannosaurus teeth.

My cousin Ralph used to have a swell tyrannosaurus necklace. I couldn't believe it when he showed up with all those teeth around his neck. Ralph is kind of a runt. I couldn't figure out how he killed a tyrannosaurus. For a guy like Ralph, the most likely way to hurt a giant dinosaur is to become a fatal bowel obstruction.

Ralph got a lot of action out of that necklace. To the point where he used to hide in my cave and suck raptor eggs to get his strength back. Then, one day, a girl pried the truth out of him. During the afterglow. He got the teeth from a tyrannosaurus that died in a rockslide. Boy, was she mad. Now she also has a necklace made from teeth. And Ralph's sister has to chew his food for him.

Shoes are all the rage now. You take a couple of thick pieces of animal hide and wrap them around your feet and tie them with leather strips, and suddenly, you aren't bothered as much by pointy things on the ground. And you look smart.

Shoes were invented a short time ago, and it was only a week later that a clever guy went one step further and invented the elevator shoe. In fact, it was my cousin Ralph, mentioned above. This was before the tyrannosaurus trick was exposed. Ralph realized that by putting rocks in the hides before tying them on, he could increase his height to a towering four feet, two inches.

The shoes weren't perfect. Because the rocks were heavy, it was exhausting to walk, so Ralph would shuffle a few feet and then rest a while, gasping for breath. And it confused the women. Here was this tall, dashing hunk with a terrific tyrannosaurus-tooth necklace, but he could only walk a couple of yards without stopping, and his arms were really short. And his crotch was nearly at eye level.

When the secret of his necklace came to light, it was the shoes that did him in. He ran about three steps before the girl knocked him over and sat on him. Also, he couldn't see where he was going, because he was wearing a badly anchored tree-rat toupee.

Actually, it was a *live* tree rat, tied on with vines, and it got loose in the struggle. And tree rats are wiry, scrappy, and extremely vindictive. Ralph might conceivably have been able to take on one angry girl, but when the tree rat threw in with her, he didn't stand a chance.

Inventive guy, Ralph. But he hasn't invented a good substitute for teeth.

Women's shoes are a problem. A guy will make himself one pair of shoes and be done with it. A woman will collect shoes until her cave is completely full and her husband has to go dig himself a burrow. Then she fills that with shoes, too.

If you ask a woman why she has fifty pairs of shoes that are all exactly alike, she puts her hands on her hips and asks how you can possibly think a midcalf wildebeest-hide shoe is remotely similar to a midcalf antelope-hide shoe with a weasel-fur collar.

This is one reason men are currently hitting the berry juice much earlier in the afternoon.

There are a few other fashion items I should mention. Like paint. Some guys find skins confining, so they grind up various berries and make paint, which they use to cover their bodies from head to toe. And they claim this counts as clothing, although to me, blue parts are still parts.

We had three blue guys who used to stand in the middle of the village doing a musical comedy act. Beating on logs and doing pratfalls and so on. They were really annoying. Fortunately, their act led to an important scientific discovery. Blue makes tyrannosauruses really, really angry. Which led to a body paint clearance sale. Down at Bob and Norm's Fashion Warehouse.

They sold out in a hurry. People knew that as long as they wore it they'd have to run from furious tyrannosauruses. But a bargain is a bargain.

We never did find a way to get rid of the blue stain where those three guys used to stand. Tyrannosauruses still run into the village and bang their heads against it.

5

Art

If It Sticks to the Cave Wall, It Counts

This would be a good place to tell you about my passion, which is art. It hasn't been around too long, and some people think it's a fad, but I think it's here to stay. If only because it's impossible to get stains off cave walls.

I know what you're thinking. You're thinking I'm going to say art was invented by a guy named Art. No, the inventor's name was Andy. He was a weird little dude with white hair that stuck out in all directions. Especially on his back.

Andy had a cave where all the loafers and freaks used to hang out, and he used to paint on the walls. Stupid paintings, I always thought. Like he'd paint the same piece of fruit four times, in a big square, using different colors for each picture. People said it was brilliant. I think he just didn't have much fruit. And may possibly have been colorblind. Maybe he figured if he painted the fruit in four different colors, one of the colors would have to be right.

Other guys started getting into art. Like Mike. He lived down the path from Andy, and he did really amazing work. One time a local religious leader—Big Ted—commissioned him to paint the ceiling of his cave. You'll read about Big Ted later.

**Jack can come to your cave and fling two
handfuls of paint at the wall and charge
you an elk.**

By "commissioned," I mean he told Mike to paint his ceiling
or else he would be *out* of commission. Due to a pounding from
Big Ted.

Mike painted all sorts of stuff up there. Big Ted, looking considerably more handsome than he does in real life. Little people
with wings. It was really impressive. And you could actually tell
what the things he painted were supposed to be.

Not all artists are like that. Our third artist, Jack, used to fling
stuff at the wall, sort of randomly. Usually when he was tanked up
on berry juice. When the stuff dried, he claimed it was art. Which
makes you wonder if the face of the latrine cliff could be considered a mural.

**The first art critic was a guy
named Bartholomew. Not
"Bart"–<u>Bartholomew</u>. He
lived with a guy named
Randolph. Not "Randy."**

Things went okay for
Andy and Jack and Mike
until about three weeks after
art was invented. Because
that's how much time passed
before the arrival of the first
art critic.

The first art critic was a guy named Bartholomew. Not "Bart"—*Bartholomew*. He lived with a guy named Randolph. Not "Randy."

Bartholomew had started out as an artist. He did portraits. He gave up after about a week because everyone he painted looked like a purple mesohippus with nine legs.

Bartholomew always wore black, and he palled around with weirdos and belonged to the Coalition to Stop Club Violence. And he didn't think much of Mike's work. He kept saying it was "representational." I think that was his way of saying you could tell what it was, and that it actually looked the way real stuff looked. If you paint a yellow banana, you're not worth fooling with. If you paint a bright red banana with feet, you're a genius.

Bartholomew said Andy's work was "divine" and "fabulous." He liked it so much he and Randolph sometimes spent the whole night at Andy's, looking at the art for hours and emerging exhausted. And for some reason, extremely disheveled.

As for Jack's art, Bartholomew said you either "got it" or you didn't. And unless you "got it," you could not be "fabulous." Although you could still be "a dear little lamb." Whatever that meant.

Because Mike's art tanked with the art establishment, he still has to go out and hunt and gather every day. On the other hand, Jack can come to your cave and fling two handfuls of paint at the wall and charge you an elk. Sometimes he doesn't even face the wall. He's that talented.

Me, I don't pretend to be a great artist. I know I'll never be as important as Andy or Jack. I just paint what I see. I think of myself more as a writer, anyway. Even though I am sober most of the time and have several friends.

Bartholomew came to see my work once. He sort of sniffed

Here I am, before I met Susan—a single guy without a care in the world.

This is me and Susan, and the kids. Makes you want to run out and get married, doesn't it?

and called me a primitive artist. I was like, "Dude. All artists are primitive."

By the way, we have started expanding the definition of "art" to include stuff like dancing and acting and so on. I already told you about theater and the blue guys. We also have other types of performers, such as comedians. One of our most famous comedians is a guy named Don. Here's a sample of his act.

You may have to read it twice. The humor is pretty sophisticated.

This is me and my friend Bill encountering a tyrannosaurus.

This is me and my late friend Bill fleeing a tyrannosaurus.

DON: (*to a* LADY *in the crowd*)

Hiya, sweetheart. Where you from?

LADY:

I live over by the quicksand pit.

DON:

The quicksand pit? Big Ball of Light love you, dear. Thanks for coming. And is this your husband?

LADY:

Yes.

DON:

Well, you're really, really ugly. And your husband is stupid. *(Crowd goes wild.)* Your kids are probably morons, and I hope you get eaten by an allosaurus. Please die in tremendous pain, you slut, and take your idiot husband with you.

LADY:

HAHAHAHAHAHAHAHA!

DON:

I say that with love. Big Ball of Light bless.

■ ■ ■

I hope I transcribed that right. It was a riot.

Maybe you had to be there.

We also have a famous comedian who does nothing but smash fruit. You go to his show and he takes a melon or something and puts it on a big rock, and then he takes a big hammer and smashes the crap out of it, and fruit bits fly out into the audience.

I never saw the humor in that, but he has a lot of fans among the less-evolved. Chimps, mainly.

Of course, they may just be showing up for the free fruit.

Not all art is beneficial and educational. I'll give you an example. We have these nuts who paint their faces white and refuse to talk. And they accost you while you're going about your life and do moronic little bits of theater. "Man trapped in an invisible cave." "Man pulling an invisible vine." "Man being eaten by an invisible tyrannosaurus." And they expect you to give them handouts. To make them go away.

We got so sick of them the High Council eventually put a bounty on them. Now the problem is greatly reduced. And on a rock face behind the Council Table, there is a little row of tiny white shrunken heads.

These guys pretend they can't talk, but when you toss them off a cliff, they have a way of coming out of their shell.

I'm trying to think if there is anything else we do that's in any way artistic. Oh, wait. Music. How could I forget? The blue guys used it when they did their act. Giving rise to the first noise ordinance.

Music began with singing. And it was invented by a woman in labor. She was delivering twins, and her husband showed his consideration by going outside to give her privacy and get away from the howling. After a day and a half, though, he ran out of berry juice and he started howling right along with her. And people walking by stopped to listen, and a couple of them started banging on rocks and trees. That was the first band.

Not long after that, the song was invented. And we came up with some wonderful standards. Here are some examples.

1. "I've Got You Under My Bearskin"

2. "Big Ball of Light, Bless the Child"

3. "You're Nobody 'Til Somebody Clubs You"

4. "Pangaea on my Mind"

5. "The Lady Is a Chimp"

Lately, though, music has really gone downhill. The business has been taken over by snot-nosed kids who wear their bearskins really low and pretend to be criminals. With annoying names like Neanderthals With Attitude.

They don't even sing any more. They just shout bad angry poetry.

I don't need musicians to yell at me and threaten me. I have a wife for that.

Critics seem to like the new music a lot, but it's too obnoxious for me. How obnoxious? Last month we had a hit called "Club My Bitch Up."

I'm hoping this garbage will go away and something better will replace it. Art has to get more sophisticated with time, right? I'm sure this junk is a momentary aberration.

6

Courtship and Mating
Tips for Dealing with the Baby Epidemic

I guess I ought to tell about mating and babies. The mating part—that I'm totally on board with. The babies—truthfully, I've never understood why women won't let us eat them. It would improve the noise situation, and while no one appreciates a good stink more than I do, whenever a baby is in the cave, I eventually find myself standing at the mouth, fanning out stench with a buffalo hide.

> **The babies—truthfully, I've never understood why women won't let us eat them.**

Here's how it works. My species comes in two basic flavors. Cavemen and cavewomen. There's a third variety—guys who never marry and earn their food doing cave-mouth treatments. And of course there are peculiar women who don't smile much and like to do their own hunting. But I digress. Damn this three-second attention span of mine.

The first two sexes are drawn to each other. Cavemen like the soft, musical sound women's voices make during the two percent of the time when they're not angry or complaining. And there's something about the way they look from the back that makes us crazy.

And why are cavewomen drawn to cavemen? Because we give them things and do all the work.

I know it sounds backward. Millions of years from now, I bet things will be totally different.

Don't get the idea that we're animals. We have all sorts of genteel, civilized ways for singles to meet and court. For example, there's the club scene. By that I mean clubbing the girl in the back of the head and draping her over a rock for a quick private ceremony. Guys who are more sophisticated get their way by loading their fiancées up with fermented berry juice. After that, the procedure is pretty similar.

Don't get the idea that we're all paternalistic and sexist and whatnot. Women call a lot of the shots. Sometimes, when a girl likes a guy, when she sees him coming, she'll stand facing a rock and close her eyes. And if he doesn't notice, she runs ahead of him and stands by the next rock.

We have a new thing called "poetry," which women seem to like a lot. If you're one of these modern guys who, for whatever reason, like the woman to be awake and consenting, this works wonders. What you do is, you recite a bunch of words to her in a clever way that suggests you are in some way interested in what goes on above her shoulders. Which is of course ridiculous. But they fall for it.

> **I saw her bending over to pick maggots off a dead stegosaurus. You put them in salad. Like capers.**

When I met Susan, I was planning to go the club route. I was dragging a mesohippus back

"Roses are red, violets are blue . . ."

to my parents' cave for lunch, and I saw her bending over to pick maggots off a dead stegosaurus. You put them in salad. Like capers. I knew I was in love. Because I kept looking at her instead of the maggots.

But Susan is a big girl, and a couple guys had already tried the club on her. It just bounced off. She used their skulls to make cups for a brassiere.

I decided to give poetry a try. I thought for a couple of seconds, then I got down on one knee, and I said this:

Roses are red,
Violets are blue.
I want to pin you down in the dirt and then fall asleep
*   on top of you.*

I know there are problems with the meter. But hey, this was like the eighth poem ever written. The first one was by a guy named Phil. Neanderthal. Flat head and all that, but an okay guy. You know. A *good* Neanderthal.

His poem was even worse. It went like this.

Oh, no, a tyrannosaurus.
Help, help. A tyrannosaurus.
Maybe if I hold real still
It won't

While I was reciting, I gave her a flower. This is another mystery about women: flowers make them insane, but they hardly even notice bigger and better-tasting items of produce, such as coconuts. Like I keep saying, women are not prized for their intelligence. Nature gave men the brains and women the boobs, and at least at this stage of evolution, it looks like a fair deal.

We were in the woods, and after I said my poem, I reached over and broke a big flower off its stem and handed it to her, and her eyes got all wet. For a minute I thought she was allergic. But it turned out she really liked it. I asked her how come it didn't get her excited two minutes ago when it was still on the plant, three feet away, and she kind of frowned and reached for a rock.

When I woke up, she was asleep on top of me.

"Okay, whatever," I thought, "We can play it this way."

Once you're married, you have to go find an empty cave. Or one whose owner sleeps too soundly to hear a guy come in with a club. Then you and the wife move in, and you go hunting every day and bring her dead animals, and hopefully, she skins them and cuts them up for you. And if you're lucky, you occasionally get some action. Until the dark day when babies start coming out of her.

Babies are a real problem. No one knows what causes them. Our scientists, who recently began to suspect a link between sudden death and club blows to the face, have a theory. They think maybe when you swallow a grub or a beetle without chewing it well, it grows in your belly and turns into a baby. So once Susan and I were married, I always made sure her grubs and beetles were dead before she ate them.

Still, she came down with babies.

Funny thing about babies—seems like men are immune. Some guys marry other men, which is something I understand completely, except for the disappointing nature of the mating. As far as I know, none of the wives have come down with babies. My cousin Stan has been with his wife, Hank, for ages, and so far, they're both baby-free. Knock on wood.

Some scientists think men are carriers. There might be something to it.

Marriages like Stan and Hank's are usually tense because it can be hard resolving the issue of who has to be the wife. In my experience, it's generally the smaller guy or whoever falls asleep first.

I'm not sure why most guys don't marry guys. Think about it. No problems with babies, and it's a two-income cave.

My theory is that babies are parasites. And they do something to the host's brain. When our first baby, Hal Junior, popped out, I said, "Great! It's out! I'll hit it with a rock, and you can roast it!" And Susan looked at me like I had said something ridiculous.

This thing had poisoned her mind somehow, and she was determined to protect it and feed it. She told me to go get a nice fur to wrap it in, or she was going to hit *me* with a rock.

I went to get the fur. I remembered our wedding day.

I remember how I first knew Susan was baby-positive. Or at least had Baby-Related Complex. She put on weight. She acted even crazier than usual.

**Because Susan is still in her baby-prone years, I have
a good supply of meat to get me through lean months.**

The odd thing about babies is that they eventually turn into,
not human beings, exactly, but children, which have the poten-
tial to become human beings. Women protect them fiercely until
they reach the child stage. Once they get there, they're fairly safe
from their fathers, because they become useful as helpers and
plesiosaurus bait.

I remember how I first knew Susan was baby-positive. Or at
least had Baby-Related Complex. She put on weight. She acted
even crazier than usual. And she made me bring her disgusting
things to eat. Like pterodactyl kidneys with mashed mulberries
instead of the usual drizzle of musk ox bile.

Maybe we seem stupid and immoral for thinking babies are a
disease that needs to be treated with a medical procedure. But
then it was only last month that our leading mathematician managed to count all the way to three. And it may have been a waste

of time, because the current consensus among experts is that three doesn't exist.

Here's a problem you will want to avoid, if you think your wife is susceptible to babies. When babies start to turn human, generally, they look sort of like the father. I don't know if this is the parasite's way of mocking us or what, but it's desirable because later in life, after you've been stepped on by a mammoth or eaten during a solstice celebration, people will look at the kid and remember what a swell guy you were and how great you tasted.

But for some reason, if you have a better-looking friend or neighbor, the kids will probably end up looking like *him*.

Be careful about that.

7

Family Life
Kids and Food—Know the Difference

Family life is pretty good. Before I started a family, I was only responsible for myself, I got up when I wanted, I did what I wanted, and I had no one else depending on me. On the other hand, it could be lonely sometimes. And when I felt amorous, I had two choices. Abstinence, or if fruit was in season, a brief session with a papaya.

Now that I'm married, I'm never lonely. Even when I wish I was. And I only have to rely on papaya maybe forty percent of the time. And because Susan is still in her baby-prone years, I have a good supply of meat to get me through lean months.

She won't let me touch them, of course. The trick is to take one out for a walk and come back and say you lost it. And then you go, "But cheer up! I caught a turkey!" And you hand it to her, cleaned and ready to cook.

It's not a perfect scheme. She always looks a little suspicious. Even during dinner.

She's not completely wrong. It's important to let a few of your kids survive, and even to feed them and take care of them. In spite of the fact that they're not totally human. Because if you let them live, a fair percentage of them will somehow become human, and then you get grandchildren. So you have twice the insurance against famine.

Children can be extremely useful if you know what to do with them. I already mentioned their status as the preeminent plesiosaurus bait. You toss them out in the river on the end of a vine, and when a plesiosaurus sees them, you reel them in as fast as possible. And the plesiosaurus follows them until its head is on the bank, and *WHAM!* you pop it with your club.

You have to pay attention. You can't be scratching yourself on a tree stump or eyeballing chimp chicks across the river. Because then the plesiosaurus will grab the kid, and you're DOL. "Dung out of luck." Unless it's a small one, in which case you may be able to pull it onto the bank. That way you can save the bait—I mean the kid—for re-use later. Although it will probably have teeth marks all over it.

If it looks like it's really getting marred up, the best thing is to just drop the rope and tell the wife it ran away. Unless you want to move permanently to the papaya patch.

I have a lot of plesiosaurus scars, myself. My dad really had an eye for the chimp chicks.

If you have kids, you'll have to drag them around to participate in kid activities. Like the Cavekid Athletic League. We divide our kids in teams and turn them loose in a big field with clubs and cute little spears. And the ones that survive get to play other teams the following week.

I think the parents enjoy this more than the kids do. They walk up and down the sidelines, shouting encouragement and screaming at the ref and getting in fights and conking each other with clubs. Sometimes they don't even notice that the kids have sat down and are now watching *them*.

We call the refs "zebras." That's because they wear zebra skins.

And because, like zebras, they tend to get pulled down on the ground and torn into pieces.

If you want your kids to survive, there is one person you want to avoid. And by that I mean the pediatrician, i.e., Dr. Ed. Last year, he started telling parents he could prevent their kids from getting childhood diseases. By drowning them.

Sometimes, I think he spends just a little too much time sampling his own medicinal herbs. Or maybe there is some other explanation for running around naked, insisting you're a pineapple.

You really don't want Dr. Ed to treat your kid for an earache, which they get about three times a week. He has a theory that bad spirits get stuck in the ears and that the way to get them out is to put a stick in one ear and push the spirits out the other. He told all the parents in the village that he wanted to do this to their kids for free, as part of a research study.

So far no one has taken him up on it. It sounds like an unconscionable waste of good bait.

Kids are not overly bright. And they have terrible memories. For example, I've been telling Hal Jr. over and over, "Whatever you do today, don't trade your little sister for a banana leaf full of raspberries again. It's plesiosaurus season." And then I come home yesterday and he has berries mashed all over his face. And Mel Stimson from down the path is over by the river, waiting for a plesiosaurus to bite down on little Jasmine.

I get so tired of buying her back. I once offered to trade Hal Jr. for her because I figured that would solve the problem. But Mel said Hal was too big and that Jasmine was just the right size. And of course he was right. That was the whole reason I wanted her returned.

I ended up trading five pairs of Susan's shoes for her, for Mel to give to his wife, Aurora. Then I came home and told Susan. This morning, the shoes were back in our cave and I heard moaning noises from the direction of Mel's place.

That worked out pretty good.

Kids can be very destructive. They have no idea how hard it is to hunt and gather and build and so on, so when they get bored, they destroy and waste things you've created or brought home or stolen.

Last week I brought home a bunch of mangoes and piled them in the cave so that they would rot and grow some nice maggots for us. Then I took little Jasmine fishing, and when we got back, Hal Jr. and his friends had had a mango war. Mangoes were dripping down the front of the cave and splattered all over the ground. I grabbed him by the shoulders and said, "You little punk. Do you think mangoes grow on trees?" And he just stared at me. Okay, point taken. But it was still a dumb thing to do.

> **Grandparents can be a godsend. When you're busy, you can drop your kids off with them and go about your business. Obviously, you have to lay down ground rules. No fattening snacks, the kids have to be in bed by sundown, and under no circumstances are they to be eaten.**

After that I collected some really excellent moose dung I was going to use to stuff a pillow made from a dead possum. I piled it up in a corner of the cave. And when I got home later that day, Hal Jr. had taken it out front and built himself a dung fort.

I can't have anything nice.

Grandparents can be a godsend. When you're busy, you can drop your kids off with them and go about your business. Obviously, you have to lay down ground rules. No fattening snacks, the kids have to be in bed by sundown, and under no circumstances are they to be eaten.

Back when my dad was alive, he scarfed one down, and there was nothing I could do because, like he said, I never said "no eating." He really ribbed me about it. "Gotcha," he kept saying. "*Gotcha.*" So now when we leave the kids with my mother or Susan's parents, we always make sure we have an understanding.

Like Dad used to say, "Eat my kids once, shame on you. Eat my kids twice, shame on me."

After that, things were always tense between him and Susan. She rarely mentioned his name. So I was surprised the last time she talked to me about him. She said, "Guess what? I saw Earl stuck in the tar pit up to his waist." And I said, "Oh no! Is he okay?" And she said, "I don't know. It was last week."

Discipline is changing. It used to be, if you did something bad, your dad would grab you by the throat and conk you on the head with a rock until you were sorry. Because being hit on the head is painful, and Dr. Ed says it doesn't do any lasting harm.

My dad used to say, "This is going to hurt me a lot more than it hurts you," and that was true because he held the rock the wrong way and always ended up mashing his fingers. He figured it was worth it, though, because like the saying goes, "Spare the rock and spoil the child."

Modern experts say the rock is barbaric and that enlightened parents only beat their kids with long strips of leather. Man, we've gotten soft and permissive. I tried it on Hal Jr. and he seemed to be taking it a little too well, and then I noticed I was hearing a loud squeaking sound every time the leather hit him.

Turned out he had tied a tree rat onto his rear end, under his bearskin. I untied it without thinking, which was a bad move because, as I have already pointed out, tree rats are obsessive about vengeance. In extreme cases, they have been known to fracas people up, run away, and then come back with friends.

When the dust cleared, we were both in pretty bad shape, and we faced a hard choice. Take our chances with Dr. Ed or risk bleeding to death from multiple rat bites.

We have one other modern punishment. It's called "grounding." When your kid acts up, you take him outside and bury him in the ground. This can be tricky because you have to be careful to bury him with the right end up.

Another big danger here is that while he's buried up to his neck thinking about what a bad kid he's been, a scavenger may come along and pop his head right off the stem. After that, there is no point in digging him out because, without the head, the rest of him will always be pretty listless.

A final note: A lot of parents are into the "childproofing" fad these days. You have to go see Bob and Norm and buy a lot of crap to childproof your cave.

I wouldn't bother. The kids always find a way back in.

8

Medicine

Trepanning and Ritual Mutilation for Dummies

We have wonderful medical care these days. Although we don't really need it. Most people are really, really healthy. Right up until a few days before they die of natural causes. Like a cold or a splinter.

Hey, like my old man always said, if there's a mild fever out there with your name on it, it's going to get you no matter what. So you might as well enjoy life and accept the fact that not everyone lives to be a grizzled old fart of seventeen. Or to put it another way: live fast, die young, and leave a tender delicious corpse. Without so much of that gamey old-guy flavor.

I'll list a few of our more advanced procedures so that future generations won't lose the benefit of our genius.

1. Curing by Fire

This one heals all sorts of things. Colds. Plagues. Even broken bones. I'll tell you how it works.

Let's say you wake up with the sniffles one day. This can be very bad, although some years the sniffles come through and only kill twenty or thirty percent of us.

If someone hears you sniffling, they go get Dr. Ed, the shaman, and they tell him there's a public-health crisis. And Dr. Ed gets

If someone hears you sniffling, they go get Dr. Ed, the shaman, and they tell him there is a public-health crisis. Then they hold you over the big communal fire until you say you feel better.

three or four big guys to serve as nurse/pallbearer/sous chefs, and each one takes an arm or leg, and they hold you over the big communal fire until you say you feel better.

The theory goes like this. Sickness is caused by bad spirits that go inside you and screw things up. And bad spirits really hate fire. So when Dr. Ed gives you the cure, the bad spirits take off.

Except the ones that cause severe burns.

You wouldn't believe how well this works. Some people start to feel better as soon as they see Dr. Ed and his volunteer nurses coming up the path.

2. Purging

Sometimes bad spirits like to hide in your tummy. Especially when you eat meat that has been lying in the sun too long. Or too many rocks. Dr. Ed says small rocks are good for your digestion; personally, I seem to do just fine without them.

When the bad spirits are in your tummy, sometimes they won't come out for days and you miss out on a lot of news because the cliff we use as a latrine serves as kind of a community bulletin board. You'll be out there hanging on to a root, with your bottom over the edge of the cliff, and the guy next to you will go, "Hey, did you know a tyrannosaurus ate those annoying blue guys?" and you'll go "No," and then the other guy tells you.

You know who really hates this? The people who live at the bottom of the cliff. For years they've been threatening to move.

If you have bad tummy spirits, you go to Dr. Ed and he makes you drink a big serving of green coconut milk. And the next day, you get caught up on all the news. And if you drink too much, you may become extremely, incredibly knowledgeable about current events. You may find yourself listening to the news every ten or fifteen minutes for a week. While the people at the bottom of the cliff throw rocks and holler, "Enough already."

3. Trepanning

This is our most sophisticated form of medical treatment. Say you have real bad headaches or you're going blind or you have, like, a pimple on your forehead. Which is a big deal when your forehead is half an inch high. These symptoms may indicate bad spirits who live in your head. And the only way to get them out is to make them a door.

That's where the trepan comes in. This is a surgical instrument, although immediately prior to surgery it may have been a discarded antelope horn that was lying on a trash heap, or which Dr. Ed was using to scratch insect bites on his rear end.

Dr. Ed's regular nurses grab you, and a fifth nurse presses your head against a rock, and then Dr. Ed takes the horn and pokes a big hole in your skull for the spirits to come out of. And

These symptoms may indicate bad spirits who live in your head. And the only way to get them out is to make them a door.

due to the risky and invasive nature of the procedure, he usually makes your family pay in advance.

Then your head is freshly vacant, plus it has a big hole which new spirits can enter at will. So Dr. Ed plugs it with something healing and protective. Like dung.

I'm not too sure this treatment works. My cousin Elmer still has headaches. In spite of three operations. Also, now he can't move the right side of his body. Dr. Ed has him scheduled for a fire cure.

It's not Dr. Ed's fault. He always issues a disclaimer. It goes like this: "Ask Dr. Ed if trepanning is right for you. Although he will do it regardless. Trepanning is contraindicated in patients who cannot pay. If you are infected with babies or afraid you may become infected, discuss with Dr. Ed whether you should use trepanning. Because trepanning is not a cure for babies. No clinical studies have been performed in pregnant women. In fact no clinical studies have ever been performed anywhere, for any reason. In a small number of patients, trepanning produces a rare side effect known as 'recovery.' In most cases, however, patients can expect results such as screaming, begging, crying, writhing, bleeding, loss of consciousness, death, and being eaten by Dr. Ed."

That's a pretty comprehensive disclaimer, not to mention accurate. Especially given that lawyers don't exist yet because we haven't fully developed the parts of the brain that facilitate lying.

4. Plastic Surgery

Dr. Ed also does cosmetic procedures, such as killing the ugly. In less severe cases, he has been able to use body modification to drive ugliness into remission. One popular elective surgery is the classic "bone through the nose" job. Other people elect to have Dr. Ed knock out every other front tooth, giving a pleasing checkerboard effect.

For a while, Dr. Ed got a lot of competition from Roy the Tattoo Guy. Roy discovered that you could prick interesting patterns into people's skin and then fill them with an attractive pigment, i.e., dung. And the pigment stayed in place, and if the patient lived, he ended up with a pretty picture on his forehead or shoulder or whatever. Which tended to draw the eye away from the nearby ugliness.

Ugly people flocked to Roy, because he got good results without too much torn flesh or discarding of body parts. But that all came to an end. The day Dr. Ed diagnosed Roy with the sniffles.

During the fire cure, Roy kept yelling that he felt just fine and he wouldn't pay. But Dr. Ed said he was doing this one pro bono.

I miss Roy, but I didn't always like his work. For example, a lot of women made him put pictures of butterflies on their rear ends, just above the cheeks, right in the middle. They thought it was sexy, and it gave men something to watch during romantic moments, because it looked like the butterfly was trying to fly away. But it seemed kind of primitive and trashy to me.

One more thing our sophisticated descendants will probably abolish.

Medical care can be really expensive. Especially when you're paying Dr. Ed to stop.

Personally, instead of a stupid rear end tattoo, I would rather see some sort of roasted drumstick tied to the back of Susan's neck. That would be sexy, nourishing, and also convenient. In the distant future, I bet all women will wear them.

Medical care can be really expensive. Especially when you're paying Dr. Ed to stop. So Bob and Norm came up with a great idea. Everyone would pay them a certain amount every month, and then when you got sick, they would pay Dr. Ed.

You would think this would have solved the problem, but for some reason, Dr. Ed started charging more than ever and doing all sorts of unnecessary treatments. Before long he was really rich. He had to hire two ladies just to process the applications to Bob and Norm. And Bob and Norm just raised their rates.

When people saw how rich Dr. Ed was, a clever guy named John came up with a way to take advantage. When people weren't satisfied with their medical treatment—and they lived to tell—he would take them before the High Council and argue that Dr. Ed owed them compensation. And medicine being what it is, he usually won. Pretty soon, he was living in Dr. Ed's cave, and Dr. Ed was practicing in a burrow, down by the river.

Here is a transciption of one of John's speeches to the High Council. He was talking about a client who couldn't talk, because Dr. Ed jammed hot coals in her mouth to cure her hiccups.

Which worked, I should add.

JOHN:

I have to tell you right now—I didn't plan to talk about this— right now I feel her. I feel her presence. She's inside me, and she's talking to you. And this is what she says to you. She says, "I don't ask for your pity. What I ask for is your strength. And I don't ask for your sympathy, but I do ask for your courage. And also, if it's not too much trouble, please make Dr. Ed give John sixteen fat bison and that cool bear-head hat he wears."

■ ■ ■

John would still be living large, or at least living, if he hadn't gone to get the bison in person. While he was there, Dr. Ed and his orderlies all agreed that they distinctly heard him sniffle.

Too bad. He had great hair.

9

Religion
Your Deep Personal Relationship with the Big Ball of Light in the Sky

You may want to know about the spiritual part of cave life. It's not all hitting each other with clubs and being eaten by huge lizards. We have a deeper, more mystical side. For example, sometimes we roast and eat each other purely for sacrificial reasons. Not just because it's raining and we don't want to go out and kill something.

Sacrifice is a weird concept. If you grab your uncle and knock his brains out and cook him over a pile of logs, you get credit for a sacrifice. Even though your uncle was the only one who actually sacrificed anything, and you and your family got a great meal, plus all of your uncle's stuff.

Seems like if you really wanted to make a sacrifice, you'd volunteer to be cooked. But that doesn't fly with the theologians, most of whom are less fanatical about their religious beliefs than they are about barbecue.

> **We used to fight a lot about our beliefs, but we found that the piles of dead bodies attracted lots of predators.**

We have a tolerant society with a number of religions. We used to fight a lot about our beliefs, but we found that the piles of dead bodies attracted lots of predators. So even if your group won in the short term, you generally ended up in a big tree with your coreligionists, trying to run off a hungry allosaurus. By pelting it with twigs.

Or, if they weren't watching their backs, with smaller guys.

I'll start with the most popular denomination and work my way down.

1. The Church of the Big Ball of Light in the Sky

This is the biggest religion of all. There is this Big Ball of Light in the sky, and it stares down at us all day and keeps us warm and helps us see. But it goes away every night. We think it's afraid of the dark. It comes back every morning. So far.

At some point in the past, a few of us started to worry that it would go away for good if we weren't nice to it. And then it would be cold all the time and we'd bump into each other and we'd have to hunt by feel. Which would lead to sad events like grabbing what you thought was an easily strangled rodent but what was really the ear of a saber-toothed tiger.

You can imagine how upset we were. "Global darkening!"

everybody was saying. "Stop global darkening before it's too late."

At first, a few guys objected, pointing out that the Big Ball's track record for coming back was really good. We held a debate, and the skeptics argued first. Then the global darkening guys presented their evidence, i.e., the sudden, brutal slaughter of all the skeptics. And a promise that the skeptics' supporters were next.

It's hard to argue with good science.

For a while, pretty much everyone converted to the Church of the Big Ball. And we worked on strategies

> **"Global darkening!" everybody was saying. "Stop global darkening before it's too late."**

to make it happy. For example, we went up on a tall hill and threw food to it. But that didn't work. Due to the shortcomings of our space program.

After that, we decided the best strategy was to keep it entertained, so it would want to hang around and watch us all day. This led to the birth of theater. We cleared out an area down near the big communal fire, and we put on the first plays. Here's what the first drama looked like:

FIRST CAVEMAN:
I love the Big Ball of Light more than you do.

SECOND CAVEMAN:
I do not love the Big Ball of Light, for I am an infidel.

FIRST CAVEMAN:
(*Crushes* SECOND CAVEMAN's *skull with a big rock.*)

SECOND CAVEMAN'S FATHER-IN-LAW:
(*to daughter*) I told you not to marry a damn actor.

■ ■ ■

We also had some wonderful comedies. Here's a great example:

FIRST CAVEMAN:
I love the Big Ball of Light more than you do.

SECOND CAVEMAN:
I do not love the Big Ball of Light, for I am an infidel.

FIRST CAVEMAN:
(*Crushes* SECOND CAVEMAN'S *skull with a big rock.*)

FIRST CAVEMAN:
Nyuk nyuk nyuk. WOOWOOWOOWOOWOOWOOWOOWOO-
WOOWOO!

■ ■ ■

One of the most famous global darkening activist/priests was a guy named Al, who thought our technology was making the Big Ball mad. Especially fire, which supposedly, the Big Ball regarded as a type of mockery. Al told us we had to move out of our caves and stop making tools and quit building fires. And a lot of people believed him, although it took a while for folks to figure out what he was talking about, because he had a terrible lisp.

Eventually, Al's popularity faded. He had received lots of donations because of his work. As a result, he had a giant cave with several mouths and piles of tools and clubs. And he always had a huge fire going out front. He said he needed all that stuff so that he would have a good facility to do research and give speeches.

Actually, he said "rethearch" and "thpeecheth." But we understood.

After a few years of standing outside in the cold, eating raw meat and bugs, some of us began to suspect that there might possibly be something hypocritical going on.

Again, we have 75-cc brains, so you can't really blame us for being slow to notice the obvious. Our brilliant descendants will be much harder to fool.

When people realized there were inconsistencies in Al's words and actions, they decided to throw him a retirement party. And he was the main dish.

I found him a little fatty. Prosperity will do that to you.

The Big Ball church is still on top, but in order to avoid future problems like the one Al had, they came up with a thing called "offsets." You can use your tools and make fire and live in your cave, but you appease the Big Ball by going outside at night and waving your backside at his nocturnal competitor, the Little Spotty Ball of Light. And the Big Ball forgives you.

Personally, I think it's kind of backward, having a church where you can sin all you want and then buy your way out of it. Reform is probably coming soon.

I guess this would be a good time to mention the second big religion.

2. The Church of the Little Spotty Ball of Light in the Sky

I'm sure you've seen the Little Spotty Ball. It's a lot like the Big Ball, but it comes out mostly at night. We think the Big Ball doesn't like it, because something eats the Little Ball once a month, a piece at a time, and the Big Ball is the only thing up there big enough to do it. But it always grows back.

Back during the global darkening craze, a bunch of guys were worried that if the Big Ball ran off, we'd have no gods at all, so they started worshiping the Little Ball at night, when the Big Ball wasn't around to see.

The Little Ball seems a lot more easygoing than the Big Ball. Every so often, while the worshippers are dancing around under it naked, it actually blushes.

Here's something weird about the Little Spotty Ball. If you take your wife outside in the summer and sit under it when it's big and round, it's easier to get her to mate with you. Especially if you have a good poem. Here's one that always works for me:

> *How do I love thee?*
> *Let me count the ways.*
> *In the dirt.*
> *Against a rock.*
> *Under a bush.*
> *And once, over by the tar pit.*
>
> *Please let me do it again.*
> *I promise not to pull your ears this time.*

3. Tedism

Tedism is a religion invented by a guy named Big Ted. As his name suggests, Ted is a pretty big guy, and early on, he realized he could make people worship him by threatening to pull their arms off and eat them.

At first, the religion was slow to get going. But then Ted went on a proselytizing campaign. You'd be walking through the clearing down by the big communal fire, and Ted would be holding some guy by the throat, giving him just enough air to quietly repeat Ted's Prayer:

> *Our Ted*
> *Which art squeezing my windpipe*
> *Ted be thy name*
> *Thy kingdom come*
> *Whatever you want be done*
> *As long as you don't kill me*
> *Give me this day*
> *My daily air*
> *And I will give you my cave and all my stuff*
> *Lead me not into your fist*
> *But deliver me from bleeding*
> *For yours is the kingdom and the power and the right*
>   *to borrow my wife*
> *Whenever you feel like it*
> *Amen*

Big Ted's church is controversial, because it's the only one that features polygamy. I'm not sure why that rankles so many people. Some scholars think it may be because the only person the polygamy applies to is Big Ted.

Tedism has a big following in the immediate vicinity of Ted, with a dropoff in popularity that seems to increase with distance.

4. Dirt Worship

This is a religion whose chief virtue is convenience. Dirt is everywhere, so whenever you feel like going to your place of worship, you look down, and bang, there you are. In church.

Dirt worshipers—or "Dirtarians"—think the dirt is our mother, and for a time, they even called it by a woman's name: Louise. I think I would have gone with something more clever. Like "Dirtrude." But nobody asked my opinion.

The idea is that plants grow in the dirt, and animals eat the plants, and we eat the animals, so the earth is like a mother feeding its children.

Women love the idea of a big powerful female deity even stronger than Big Ted, so dirt worship attracts a lot of them. Like they needed one more reason to be crazy.

Once they saw women converting, a lot of men joined and became Dirtarians and pretended to love Louise, too. For some reason, Dirtarian girls are really easy, so the guys would stay in the church as long as they could stand it. Or until the girls became infected with babies.

Dirt worship causes a lot of problems. For one thing, there are a lot of things we normally do on the ground that Dirtarians can't do. Because it's like you're doing it on Louise's face. So when they feel the urge, Dirtarians have to wade out into the river.

This is a problem for a couple of reasons. First, it causes friction when the people downstream drink the water and notice the funny taste. Second—and this is probably more significant—swimming hasn't been invented yet.

This is why none of our faiths involve baptism. Anymore.

We've been working on technology to save people from drowning. We've noticed there are a lot of rocks on the banks of the river, so we have a theory that if you tie a rock to yourself before going in the water, it will eventually pull you up on dry land.

So far the results are discouraging.

Our scientists think it takes lots of power to pull a person through the water. So probably, we need to use bigger rocks.

5. Atheism

We have one atheist. His name is Hitch. Hitch says he is too sophisticated to believe there is a god. And he shows his sophistication by standing on a big rock while people walk to services. Flinging dung at them.

Fortunately, he usually misses. Because he precedes his flinging sessions with several generous servings of fermented berry juice. There are those who suspect that if not for the juice, the flinging would be greatly curtailed. Albeit more accurate.

Hitch says religion causes all the world's problems. But I think you could argue that some of the world's problems are caused by the type of person who flings dung.

For a guy who doesn't believe there is a god, Hitch seems to spend an awful lot of time making faces and obscene gestures at the Big Ball of Light in the Sky.

Another weird thing is, it drives him crazy that other people aren't atheists, too. Only Big Ted has a more vigorous soul-winning program.

Here's an example of how Hitch talks to believers.

HITCH:
Where do you ignorant sods think you're going?

FIRST BELIEVER:
We're going to go sing to the Big Ball of Light so it will love us and come back in the morning!

HITCH:

$&#%%#^$ THE BIG BALL OF LIGHT!!! *(Flings dung, misses.)*

SECOND BELIEVER:

How can you be so hostile to the Big Ball of Light?

HITCH:

The Big Ball of Light is a$^%*#%$^%#^%*#^#*^%##(#8!!!!! Besides, it doesn't exist!

FIRST BELIEVER:

What's that, then? *(Points at Big Ball of Light.)*

HITCH:

YOU KNOW WHAT I MEAN YOU STUPID PROLE! *(more dung)* HOLD STILL SO I CAN HIT YOU!

SECOND BELIEVER:

We *are* holding still.

HITCH:

(genuinely surprised) Blimey! *(Passes out, falls off rock.)*

■   ■   ■

For a long time, Hitch made everybody really miserable. Then one day he made the mistake of blaspheming Big Ted. And word was eventually passed to Ted Himself. And by "eventually passed," I mean about fifty people trampled each other, running to tell Him. And Ted decided it was time to interrupt His busy schedule by giving Hitch a little spiritual counseling. Applying the rod or, more accurately, the fist, of correction.

Like Ted's Twenty-second Proverb says, "Folly is bound up in the heart of a non-Tedist, and the fist of correction shall drive it far from him. Along with his teeth."

Ted hasn't caught Hitch yet, but at least the dung-flinging has stopped. And if He ever does catch him, Bob and Norm are giving very high odds in favor of conversion.

10

Government
You Groom My Back and I'll Groom Yours

I suppose you'll want to know about our system of government. We're even prouder of it than the latrine cliff. In fact, many people say that dealing with the government is a lot like living at the base of the cliff.

Our system of government has three branches. We call them "branches" because when we first came up with the idea of government, we were still living in trees. And people in one part of the government all tended to sit on the same branch. Well, they didn't sit so much as sleep. You know government workers.

First, we have the executive branch. They make all the important day-to-day decisions and it's their job to declare war on other villages. Then there is the legislative branch. They sit around making up new laws, like the one ban-

The main part of the executive branch is the High Council. This is a bunch of old guys who sit around picking ticks off each other and telling the rest of us what to do.

ning keeping tyrannosaurus puppies as pets. Finally, there is the nagging branch. This is a branch made up completely of women,

When we first came up with the idea of government, we were still living in trees. And people in one part of the government all tended to sit on the same branch.

and their job is to show up and criticize the other branches. The other two branches were planned, but this one sort of formed spontaneously.

For a time we had a judicial branch, but we eventually decided bribing three branches of government was too big a drain on the economy.

The main part of the executive branch is the High Council. This is a bunch of old guys who sit around picking ticks off each other and telling the rest of us what to do. Some have been in power so long they're actually in their midteens.

The High Council sits in a place of honor down by the big communal fire, approving laws, resolving disputes, and mostly taking bribes. They collect a certain amount of revenue in taxes, but bribes are really what make the system go. And the two big sources of bribes are a local "businessman" named Walkenopithecus and, of course, Bob and Norm's Lobbying Service.

A lobbyist is a person who takes your bribe to the politician for you. Originally, anyone could walk right up to a civil servant and give him a handful of grubs or a sturdy surplus daughter. That was before Bob bribed the legislative branch to pass a law requiring lobbyists to have a license.

Walkenopithecus got a special exemption from the licensing law by having his boys smear Bob and Norm with honey, roll them in ants, and dangle them over the lair of an anteater. I don't know what anteaters will be like in the future, but right now they're about the size of two mastodons and they are not all that stringent on the "ants only" thing.

At first Bob and Norm said they couldn't compromise their integrity by lobbying for an unfair law benefiting a special interest other than themselves. But they began to see the merit of Walkenopithecus's argument when the anteater stomped out of its lair and took down a palm tree with its thirty-foot-long, highly abrasive tongue. Walkenopithecus said he didn't want to push them and told them to take all the time they needed to make a good decision. And luckily he became convinced they had made the right choice while Bob and Norm still had a good deal of skin left.

The one branch of of government you can't bribe is the nagging branch. Don't get me wrong. Women will take absolutely anything you give them and still feel cheated. But you can't alter their criticizing and complaining by paying them off. Because they don't do it out of greed. They do it for pleasure.

Sex . . . now *that* they do out of greed.

One time, the High Council declared war on another village because they were kidnapping and eating an unreasonable number of our children. Which are very useful around the cave. And the nagging branch sent their delegate, Cindy, to criticize.

Boy, did Cindy let them have it. Here is a partial list of reasons she claimed the executive branch had gone to war.

1. To steal the other village's firewood supply and sell it through Bob and Norm for kickbacks.

2. To punish the other village for trying to eat the High Council President's dad.

3. To mask their sexual inadequacies, which Cindy knew about, because her girlfriends had slept with most of them. Almost as much as they had with each other.

4. To please the patriarchal, gynophobic Big Ball of Light in the Sky, which Cindy and her friends considered ridiculous because, as everyone knew, the real god was Louise.

5. Because they were men, and men are stupid.

Then Cindy and her friends did something really awful. Something we all dread. They dropped their clothes and continued their protest in the nude. They always do that when they're really upset.

It was a cruel gesture and also pointless, since the High Council was now too busy heaving and retching to conduct business. And the smell attracted a pack of hyenas.

Bob and Norm decided to persuade Dr. Ed to give Cindy a fire cure, but unfortunately she got wind of it and ran off to a village where the people are really rude and dirty and only eat snails.

The rest of the gals were happy to see Cindy go, because toward the end of her time here, she had begun to innovate. She had begun using her nagging powers on other naggers. Like if they didn't hate the war enough, Cindy would take off her clothes and nag the life out of them. Which caused internal strife and also exacerbated the village's problems by drawing flies and vultures.

The naggers thought it was great when she only nagged the High Council, the legislative branch, random men, and certain trees. But nagging other naggers . . . that was a disturbing breach of professional courtesy.

You can imagine the problems that arise from relying on polls taken in 5 million B.C., when the smartest people around are only marginally more clever than fish.

One big problem with the High Council is that it is getting too poll-driven. You can imagine the problems that arise from relying on polls taken in 5 million B.C., when the smartest people around are only marginally more clever than fish. Also, the results are highly unreliable, because we can't count high enough to tabulate them. The President will ask an aide what a poll says, and the aide will go, "A whole bunch of people are against dung subsidies." And the President will go, "Well, who is for them?" And the aide will go, "Another bunch of people." And the President will go, "Well, which bunch of people is bigger?" And the aide will go, "They all looked roughly the same size."

The legislative branch has supreme power to pass and enact

laws. Almost. Because the President has to approve everything
they do. And if they pass a law he doesn't like, he quashes it by
sending a big guy named Vito over to mash a few of their skulls.
He calls this "exercising the Vito power."

Vito has a cousin, also named Vito. He's really short. While
Big Vito clubs the legislator's heads, his cousin bites them in the
leg. Everyone calls him the Pocket Vito.

The executive branch controls the military, if "control" is really
the accurate word. It's not easy to convince guys to go to war. A
recruiter has to sit them down and say, "Okay, we need you to go
to this other village and crack skulls, and obviously, the people
from the other village will kill a few of you. Or, let's not kid ourselves, maybe all of you. But we will wait here and cheer you on.
In total safety. With your wives and girlfriends. Who will probably be pretty lonely. Also the pay stinks."

It's not what I would call an easy sell.

The obvious danger is that the recruits will be more scared of
the enemy than they are of the High Council. So every year we
have a holiday where we celebrate our soldiers. By eating a few.
That does wonders for morale.

We have tried to get along with other villages. For a while
we had a thing here where they sent their representatives, and
we tried to hammer out agreements in the interest of peace. We
called it the United Villages.

It didn't work out too good. We donated some caves and some
land, and we provided a security detail, and the foreign ambassadors repaid us by spending every day giving speeches on what
jerks we were and how great it would be if we all died and they
got our women.

They tried to pass all sorts of agreements limiting our industry.
For example, they tried to tell us only "developing villages"

could build fires and make wheels because fires burned up all the trees, and wheels were depleting the world's rock reserves.

Our High Council tried to solve the problem. By sending an appropriate ambassador, i.e., Big Ted. It worked great for a while. They shut up about the unfair agreements, and a good percentage of them became devout Tedists. But then the nagging branch showed up and paraded around naked until the High Council agreed to withdraw Big Ted and nominate someone more in line with the UV's position. Which was that we were the scum of the earth and ought to be annihilated.

We ended up sending a guy named Jimmy. He had had quite a few trepannings, so he didn't say a hell of a lot. He just grinned with his big teeth and tittered and voted yes. Even when the UV wasn't in session.

Eventually there was an accidental fire and rockslide and flood of boiling tar from somewhere above the caves, and the UV was destroyed. A few foreign ambassadors managed to run out of the complex, but unfortunately, they were all accidentally tackled and hit in the head with stone axes thirty or forty times. Or however many hits it took.

The High Council plans to rebuild the UV real soon, only they have to see a cave-impact study before that can happen, and the legislature has to fund the study, and that means endless debates and speeches, and honestly, we don't know when all this stuff will be finished.

Just in case it comes together, we are trying to train Jimmy to vote no.

11

Hazards of Caveman Life
The Importance of Not Being Swallowed Whole

Cave life is full of danger. Seems like every time I sit down to a meal with the family, someone is missing. If Susan weren't highly susceptible to infection with babies, we would probably be all by ourselves. I think there must be something wrong with her immune system.

I'll go into a little more detail about the dangers we face every day.

1. Tyrannosauruses

This has to top the list. To a tyrannosaurus, a village is like a big self-stocking meat store.

There are a few things you can do to make yourself safer. The main idea is to make yourself less appetizing than your neighbors. Or, if it's easier, to make your neighbors more appetizing than you. There are a number of ways to do this. One easy way is to make your neighbors smell like something tyrannosauruses really love to eat. Like a uintatherium. They gobble those like nuts.

So what you do is, you get yourself a uintatherium and cook it, and when your neighbors go to sleep, you run over to their cave and smear the fat all around the mouth. Of course, a tyrannosaurus may smell you while you're on the way over there with the fat. In which case, the trick fails to pay off.

Another great trick is to paint your neighbors blue, which, as I have noted earlier, makes tyrannosauruses absolutely furious. The problem with this trick is that it lacks subtlety. The neighbors may not notice a little fat on the mouth of their cave, but when you start grabbing them and smearing them with blue paint, they usually realize the gloves are pretty much off.

Some people claim a tyrannosaurus won't eat you if you hold still, because they can only see things that move. This is a myth. I know this because I did an experiment. I told a neighbor's kid I would give him two coconuts if he stood outside my cave for half an hour, totally motionless, holding a big piece of uintatherium liver. Which I had painted blue.

At least I got to keep my coconuts.

2. Velociraptors

These are sort of like tyrannosauruses, but they're smaller, faster, and above all, smarter. For example, if you take a rock and put uintatherium fat on it, a velociraptor will lick the fat off. Instead of eating the rock.

Pretty much the only way to survive a velociraptor attack is to not be the slowest person in the area. Therefore a good rule of thumb is, when you suspect there are velociraptors around, go up to the fattest guy you can find, lift a big rock over your head, and bring it down on his toes. Make sure you get away clean, because otherwise the fat guy may grab you and, while the velociraptors approach, sit on you out of spite.

Personally, I think that is just childish.

When you suspect there are velociraptors around, go up to the fattest guy you can find, lift a big rock over your head, and bring it down on his toes.

3. Disease

Notice I just say "disease" without getting any more specific. That is because as far as I know, virtually all diseases except babies are fatal. And the ones that aren't fatal on their own often become so. With the help of our local physician, Dr. Ed. Maybe I should put him on this list.

4. The Tar Pits

The tar pits are a fine source of tar and reasonably fresh meat. However, each year, they claim a surprising number of hominid lives. Because once your feet are in the tar, you sink and sink until finally only the top of your head sticks out. Luckily, this may take days, so you get time to wrap up your business and make a graceful exit, and your family and friends can come and keep you company while you sink. Generally, you are better off with your family than your friends, because your blood relatives will be more inclined to reach you a stick and try to pull you out. If it's just friends and neighbors, they are more likely to remain on the bank, fighting over who gets the drumsticks.

5. War

Every so often, we have a problem with a neighboring village. Like the time the people just north of us started blocking the paths to the best areas to forage for dung.

> **And so began the war, also known as Operation Enduring Dung.**

The High Council got together and had meetings, and they decided we had to go to war to protect our dung supply. So they sent out recruiters with the following patriotic message: "Fight for us and possibly survive and be honored for a couple of days and then ignored, or dodge the draft and be pummeled with a big club and turned into stew." And so began the war, also known as Operation Enduring Dung.

Naturally, anti-war nuts like Cindy got naked and started marching around the communal fire, chanting "No blood for dung." And a lot of the Dirtarians started complaining that we needed to end our dependence on foreign dung. Although they wouldn't let us dig up our own unused dung areas, because they said Louise didn't like it. And oddly, a lot of them were huge dung consumers.

Then one of the guys on the council—Dick was his name—noted that we could make a good substitute for dung by composting Dirtarians. And resistance to the war dropped off in a hurry, and Cindy put her clothes back on, and for the first time in days, we were all able to enjoy our food.

The secret to surviving military service is to do really excellent and impressive aggression displays while remaining at least a hundred yards from the actual fighting. When it's over, most of the guys who know that you didn't actually help will be dead, and you'll be swimming in chicks. And then the spoils will be divided up, and hopefully, you'll get a profitable dung distribution contract. Or something.

6. Primate Unexplained Death Syndrome (PUDS)

This one covers most of the hazards not mentioned above. We have a lot of inexplicable casualties that take us completely by surprise.

I'll give you a good example. Say you're on top of a cliff. And your buddies are down below, and they wave at you and you decide to join them. So you jump off the cliff, and you're fine for the first hundred feet or so, but then for some reason, as you hit the bottom, the situation deteriorates rapidly. I mean, one second, you're healthy and strong and you're looking forward to seeing your pals, and the next second, you're a big dead pile of raw meat and your buddies are scooping you into pouches to take home. We lose several guys every year that way.

Here's another one that happens a lot. A guy has an argument with his wife, and maybe he smacks her a couple of times to knock some sense into her. And she sees that he's right, and they make up and go to bed. And when morning comes, she's fine, but he doesn't get up, because his head is mashed in. At bedtime, fine. In the morning, head all mashed. A puzzle.

Dr. Ed has been trying to figure out what causes it. He thinks maybe it's some kind of giant mosquito, attracted by the sounds of people arguing. But it also happens to couples who argue quietly.

Funny how it only strikes men.

7. Walkenopithecus

Walkenopithecus is a local guy. Some years, he causes more deaths than all other hazards combined. But the victims always have it coming. Like, say, a guy nails an apatosaurus and brings the carcass home and doesn't give Walkenopithecus a taste. Or a guy opens a business and he fails to pay Walkenopithecus a fee to make sure it doesn't succumb to one of those crazy fluke disasters, like being burned down and shoved into the tar pit. Whenever you do anything in the village that involves the possibility of profit, you have to remember, at the top of your to-do list, to put "pay Walkenopithecus."

We think a certain number of PUDS deaths are actually attributable to Walkenopithecus. But it's hard to tell. Like when you find bits of a guy strewn up and down a path near his new business, which he didn't tell Walkenopithecus about. Maybe Walkenopithecus did it. On the other hand, maybe the deceased was depressed. And therefore cut himself in tiny pieces and distributed them over a couple of acres.

These scientific questions can be very tough to resolve. Especially when Walkenopithecus volunteers his boys, Benny and Seymour, to help with the investigation.

They do great work, but it seems like whenever they're involved, the other investigators suffer a really high incidence of on-the-job PUDS.

Walkenopithecus is so feared, even Big Ted pays him. One

time a worshiper asked Big Ted why, if he was god, he paid protection money to a mere man. And Big Ted rolled him up sort of like an animal skin and stuffed him sideways into a knothole. And all the other followers gathered around and stared at him, figuring it had to be some sort of parable or riddle.

Ted loves riddles. For example, he loves to ask people, "What is the sound of one hand clapping?"

Then he slaps you.

He's a witty guy for a mystic.

Anyway, life is very dangerous, so I suppose that on balance, the baby plague isn't an entirely bad thing. And when life is over, you get to go be with the Big Ball of Light in the Sky. Where you always have plenty of meat and berry juice. Not to mention a fabulous tan.

12 🔥

Walkenopithecus

Researcher's Note: At one point in the picture record, there is a section painted in a different hand. Upon ingesting the appropriate medications and deciphering the images, I realized I had a bloody wonderful find. A second caveman had interrupted Hal to write down his thoughts. Here is what he had to say.

Hi, future humans. Call me Chris. Thought I'd scratch down a few things while Hal recovers from a nose piercing.

Hal told you about other guys in the village, yes? Dr. Ed. Cousin Ralph. Roy the tattoo guy—Big Ball of Light rest his soul. You might want to hear about me. If it's not too boring.

I suppose you want to know what I do. "Business," I would call it. Is it necessary to be specific? Fine. A little of this. And sometimes a little of that. Allow me to elaborate.

Got a couple of boys who work for me. Benny and Seymour. They do the heavy lifting. That stuff is not for me, because I am an executive. I am management. I do not sweat.

That is a rule. Like the rule that if you interrupt me twice during a sales pitch, I have Benny make your head into a wall-mounted torch holder.

Good rules make for good business. You agree, surely? You would if you were here right now. People invariably agree with me when we deal face-to-face. Or, in difficult cases, face to foot. Or face to red-hot coals fresh from the fire.

I'll explain what it's like to be in management. Say a guy gives me a bison. Because he is so glad and so grateful that nothing bad will happen to his wife and kids and parents and home and business during the coming month. I kiss him on both cheeks and tell him I appreciate the gift. And that I look forward to another gift at the beginning of the next month. Which will also be uneventful. But Benny and Seymour are the ones who actually drag the bison home.

A lot of what I do is in the nature of security. You want your home or business to be secure? You better pay me. I'm not saying they won't be secure if you don't. I'm just saying . . . things happen. Seems like a week never goes by when a search doesn't turn up people who could not be persuaded to buy my services.

Not really people. Parts of people.

The charges are not extravagant, mind you. I am a

reasonable man. I charge on a sliding scale. You live in a hole with a palm frond over the top? I am happy with a bimonthly lizard and a few grubs. You live in a fancy cave with four mouths and its own spring? Oh, my friend. I'm afraid you are going to have to pony up a bison. Monthly. Minimum. Otherwise Benny and Seymour climb out on a branch over the river and dangle you for the mosasauruses. When they are finished, we pull up the rope and try to strike a deal with whatever remains at the end of it.

I have a slogan. "From each according to his ability . . . to Chris." I wrote that myself. If you use it, you have to credit me. I may be dead, but I'll have descendants.

I'll give you an idea what a typical business meeting is like. Last week I went to see Dr. Ed. Because I heard he trepanned a guy and took a fee and didn't give me a taste.

I tell you freely, my feelings were hurt. I thought Dr. Ed and I were friends. Amigos. Brethren. He came to me for a loan when he first opened his practice. Needed a few instruments and medications. Mostly pointy rocks and dung.

I told Benny and Seymour to give him what he needed, and I put my arm around him, and I said this to him. "Ed . . . Edward . . . Eddie . . . may I call you Eddie? It suits you. To some you may be fearsome, but to me you have a quality I would almost describe as puckish. Anyway, Eddie, the thing is this. I respect your grift. The doctor act? Genius. Class-A work. People get sick, you burn them in the fire, you cut off a leg, you install a bay window in a forehead, and they die. Which would have happened anyway. But thanks to you, during the course of the illness, a few skins and tools and shells enter the stream of commerce and benefit the local economy. Everybody wins. Except the dead mark, who, regardless, was going to get kacked. We both know this."

He seemed perturbed. He had not realized I grasped the subtleties of his art.

"Anyway," I told him, "I am not here to point out the obvious. Which is that with all your knowledge and arcane skills, you could not cure a rat if its ass fell asleep. What I am here to tell you is this. Some day, and that day may never come, a relative or close friend of mine may call upon you to do a service for them. Such as a prophylactic amputation. And you are to turn them away. Because if anyone I care about comes home with a missing arm or a hole in his head packed with dung, I will have to come to your place of business with Benny and Seymour and perform exploratory surgery. On you. With the dullest stick on the premises. Am I understood?"

Oh, I was understood. To the point where Dr. Ed generated a particularly handsome stool sample.

Flattering.

I continued. "There are seventeen different things a

guy can do when he's scared, to give him away. A guy has seventeen pantomimes. And that," I said, pointing to the sample, "is one of them."

I stepped over it and went home, after telling Ed the juice on his loan was already running. And I thought that was the end of it.

Silly me. Last week my neighbor Sid went in with a sinus headache, and Ed opened him up like a pomegranate, and I never saw so much as a clamshell.

I could have warned Sid. But he is not the greatest neighbor in the world. He buttonholes me outside my cave and talks to me for hours about his feet. Like I have nothing better to do. Look, if your feet are sore, quit swinging from them. Simple, no? But he would not listen. So now when you put your ear up against his temple, you can hear the ocean.

And thankfully, nothing else.

I rounded up Benny and Seymour, and we went over to give Dr. Ed a sort of reverse house call. He had some lady on the exam rock, and she had a sprained ankle, and he was getting ready to fix things. By taking off the leg. And we walked in, and I tossed her a handful of beads and told her to limp herself the hell out of there and forget the address. Which, as Hal has noted, is not hard when you have an IQ of 27 and could make a fine roomy hat out of a walnut shell.

"Eddie," I said, fingering an especially large and nasty-looking stone knife, "what can you tell me about these memory problems you've been having? Like, I heard you trepanned a guy. And you forgot I was entitled to fifteen percent. <u>And</u> that you liked having your intestines on the inside."

At this point, he became belligerent. Truculent, even. He told me he was now a businessman, too. He said he had a staff of brawny male nurses, and if I didn't get out of his office, he would call for them and they would give me a fire cure to get me over the sniffles. Which he was sure I was catching, because I sounded quite nasal.

"Nurses?" I asked him. "Oh, you mean my new associates. Who are down by the river enjoying a nice barbecue my people prepared for them. With their skin bags full of their first week's pay. You mean those nurses?"

This time, the pantomime was even more vigorous. It bounced. Twice.

I continued. "So, Eddie. Time for a second opinion. Do you still think I need a fire cure, or is it possible you would like to rekindle our friendship pretty much on its former terms?" And he made the right choice. Smart boy, Eddie. After all, he's a doctor.

I decided we should celebrate our new understanding with a toast. So Benny and Seymour grabbed Eddie and held him over the fire. And toasted him a little.

And because our spirits were so light, we sang a little song. And not surprisingly, Eddie sang loudest of all. If poorly.

I had to dance. I have always been a dancer at heart. And because the office had a sand floor, I decided to give Eddie a little bit of the old soft shoe. I picked a good time for it. Shoes were invented the previous month. Before that, we called it "the old soft foot." Which didn't really make much sense.

So. Now you know a little about me. I hope you were entertained. It is time to make my exit, for I have learned that a couple of gonifs in the village are selling sticks without cutting me in on the profits. One is named Bob and the other, Norm. Short guy, short, fat guy. Not sure if they're a couple or what. Maybe they're dodging the baby plague.

In matters of romance, I do not judge. Regardless if a pair's appearance gives rise to amusing mental images.

In matters of business, I judge. Oh, do I judge.

They have some kind of home-improvement grift. I will tell them they can improve their homes by taking valuable stuff out of them and turning it over to me. Otherwise . . . buckwheats. By that I mean we tie them up in a field of buckwheat. And set it on fire.

They put on seminars. I'll put on one of my own. "This Old Cave. Today's episode: 'Free Sticks for Everybody While Bob and Norm Get Buckwheats.' "

At times I find the showman in me irrepressible.

That is my story. I hope you will understand me correctly, and that future hominids will think well of me.

Or alternatively, that my descendants will convince them to think well of me. By judicious applications of buckwheats.

Now I am off to see those grasping stick merchants. Big Ball of Light help them.

13

Never Drag a Woman by Her Hair Extensions
Tips On Finding Your Inner Caveman

Note: This chapter is a first-person account written by the author, Steve H. Graham.

Like most people, I found Dr. Drambuie-Mason's discoveries shocking and sensational. But I didn't realize Hal's diaries were only part of the story. To help you understand what I mean, allow me to detail an experience Drambuie-Mason and I shared in a diner just outside Chicken Bend.

We were trying to get breakfast after a tiring morning of collation and editing, and apparently, we missed the 11 A.M. deadline. By a remarkable stroke of luck, I happened to have my voice recorder running. Here is what it picked up.

DR. DRAMBUIE-MASON:
. . . so my contention is, even if it *was* found in my luggage, I had just returned from a dig in the New Mexico desert, where peyote grows wild. And there is every chance that the wind simply blew it into my effects.

ME:

What about the peyote residue they found in the enema bag?

DR. DRAMBUIE-MASON:

My dear fellow. The wind outside Flagstaff is something you really must see to understand.

WAITRESS:

Good morning! Can I get y'all something to drink?

DR. DRAMBUIE-MASON:

(feeling around in his briefcase) I don't suppose you have tonic water?

WAITRESS:

Afraid not, sugar.

DR. DRAMBUIE-MASON:

(sighs) Tea, then.

WAITRESS:

Sweet tea?

DR. DRAMBUIE-MASON:

What in blazes is that?

ME:

I'll have an RC.

WAITRESS:

Got any idea what y'all want?

DR. DRAMBUIE-MASON:
I'd like two soft-boiled eggs and a bit of toast.

WAITRESS:
Sorry. *(Points at clock.)*

DR. DRAMBUIE-MASON:
I say!

ME:
Guess we lost track of time.

WAITRESS:
How about some nice chicken and waffles?

ME:
Yes. Extra gravy, please.

DR. DRAMBUIE-MASON:
But dash it . . . I haven't had breakfast.

ME:
Got any pie back there?

DR. DRAMBUIE-MASON:
See here, my good woman. It's only five past. Surely you could
see your way clear to—

WAITRESS:
I can get you some egg salad!

DR. DRAMBUIE-MASON:

Blast your egg salad!

ME:

Can we have separate checks?

WAITRESS:

Now just a daggone minute . . .

WAITRESS:

Y'all ain't from around here, are you?

ME:

I'll take mine to go.

(*At this point,* DRAMBUIE-MASON *jumps on to the table, squats on his haunches, and begins making hooting noises while rubbing mustard into his hair.*)

■ ■ ■

The remarkable thing is, after putting on this bizarre display, Drambuie-Mason got exactly what he ordered. The cook boiled him some eggs and made him some toast, and we paid for our meal and left without incident. Because no one in the place knew what to do with him. They were so nonplussed, they decided the best thing was to give him what he wanted and hope he didn't have a full-blown seizure.

As we drove back to his camp near the caves, with the mustard forming a hard crust we would later have to remove with a masonry hammer, Drambuie-Mason explained. He said that ever since he had begun reading about caveman society, he had realized that many of their customs could have wide application to modern life. And over the years he had been trying it, with great success. Naturally, I was fascinated, and I proceeded to interview him extensively on the subject. I'll give you a few of his ideas.

1. Around the House

Imagine this. It's Sunday. It's football season. Your team is in the playoffs. Which means, unlike me, you don't live in Miami. If you will pardon the digression.

You're all prepared. The day before, you bought beer and chips and dip and salsa. The kids are at your wife's parents' house. The game comes on in three minutes. And you just ordered a pizza.

And your wife comes in and stands between you and the TV and says you're going to Home Depot to look at tile.

According to Dr. Drambuie-Mason, modern women, though somewhat brighter than their distant forebears, are still motivated largely by atavistic drives that were well established in Hal's time. And whether they know it or not, they do annoying things primarily in order to provoke a primitive response they claim to hate but actually find strangely satisfying. Your wife may think she's trying to motivate a fat lazy oaf to get off the couch so she can go stare at three thousand different floor tiles, which she knows look exactly alike to him. In reality, she is giving you a sort of primitive testosterone test to see if you can sire vigorous spawn.

There are two ways to handle this. First, the modern way.

WIFE:

Turn that off. We're going to Home Depot to look at floor tiles, and after that you can hold my purse and look lost while I try on forty-seven nearly identical pairs of shoes.

HUSBAND:

I would really rather watch the game, but I'm a man, so I guess I must be wrong. Let me drive you to the mall in the tan minivan you made me buy instead of the cool hemi pickup I liked. We'll put Melissa Etheridge in the CD player, and I'll apologize over and over for being insensitive about your needs.

WIFE:

(looking out the window) Looks like rain.

HUSBAND:

Really? I'm sorry!

WIFE:

What is it about you that makes you so disappointing?

HUSBAND:

(crying) I bet Oprah would know.

■   ■   ■

Here, according to Dr. Drambuie-Mason, is the correct way to satisfy your wife's inner needs:

WIFE:

Turn that off. We're going to Home Depot to look at floor tiles, and after that you can hold my purse and look lost while I try on forty-seven nearly identical pairs of shoes.

HUSBAND:

(Grunts, snarls, picks up club, shatters glass coffee table.)

WIFE:

My table! Hey, where did you get that club? It's kind of . . . sexy.

HUSBAND:

(staring at her legs) Woman look nice. *(Opens shirt and begins rubbing dip on chest.)*

WIFE:

What has gotten into you today? Have you been listening to Ted Nugent again?

HUSBAND:

(coming toward her with bowl of dip in hand) Woman too much talk, too much clothes!

WIFE:

(raising skirt, showing him a knee) Maybe we could look at tile some other time . . .

HUSBAND:

GRRRRRRRRRR . . . *(Lunges for her.)*

WIFE:

(She ducks, then runs.) RACE YOU TO THE BEDROOM!

■ ■ ■

This also works when you get invited to a baby shower. I have no idea why people invite men to baby showers, knowing it's incredibly tacky and inappropriate. Well, yes I do. They want gifts. If you actually show up, it kind of freaks them out.

In any case, if you master this tactic, instead of running a lot of miserable errands and suffering through boring social events, you'll get to stay home, damaging your dinner table's finish with sweat puddles shaped like your wife's back.

2. At the Mall

Imagine this scene. You go to a store and buy a new cellphone. And you're supposed to get a rebate. You take your phone home, and you open the package, and you plug the phone into the wall charger. And—surprise—no rebate form. What do you do? Most likely, you slink back to the store, wait for a pimply clerk to make eye contact, and whimper for mercy.

Unfortunately, that's exactly what they expect.

YOU:

(as pimply clerks flit by) Excuse me . . . excuse me . . . excuse me . . . excuse me . . .

(After 15 minutes of this, a KID *with a ring in each nostril decides he has time to talk to you.)*

YOU:

Excuse me . . .

KID:

What?

YOU:

I just bought this phone, and there was supposed to be a rebate form, and I got it home and there was no form in the box.

KID:

That sucks, dude. Have a nice day.

YOU:

No, wait. I mean, how can I get a rebate form?

KID:

Not our problem. Talk to the manufacturer.

YOU:

But I just bought it.

KID:

That sucks, dude.

YOU:

I realize it sucks. I figured that out on my own. Can't you fix it?

KID:

Let me talk to my manager. *(Goes over to video game area, plays Grand Theft Auto with older pimply kid for 15 minutes, comes back.)*

YOU:

Well?

KID:

Kicked his ass.

YOU:

What about my rebate?

KID:

Not our problem. Talk to the manufacturer.

YOU:

Is that what your manager told you?

KID:

I didn't actually mention you.

YOU:

Why not?

KID:

I was hoping you'd get tired and go home.

YOU:

Oh, God.

KID:

Have a nice day.

■ ■ ■

That's the modern way. Here's the caveman way:

YOU:
(as pimply clerks flit by) UGH! UGH! UGH! UGH!

(After 30 seconds of this, a pimply KID *with a ring in each nostril comes within club range. You bonk him with your club.)*

YOU:

(BONK)

KID:

OW!!!

YOU:

(BONK)

KID:

OW! STOP HITTING ME!

YOU:

WANT REBATE!

KID:

That's not our problem! Talk to the manufacturer!

YOU:

(BONK)

KID:

OW! WAIT! WAIT! WAIT! LET ME GET MY MANAGER! HECTOR, CAN YOU COME TALK TO THIS GUY?

HECTOR:

I'm the manager. How can I help you?

YOU:

WANT REBATE!

HECTOR:

Have you contacted the manufacturer?

YOU:

(BONK)

HECTOR:

OW!

KID:

HAHAHAHAHA!

YOU:

(BONK)

KID:

OW!

YOU:

(BONK)

HECTOR:

OW!

YOU:

(BONK)

KID:

OW!

YOU:

(BONK)

HECTOR:

OW!

YOU:

GRRRRRRR! *(beginning a backswing for a fresh bonk)*

HECTOR:

WAIT! WAIT! I HAVE A HUNDRED BUCKS IN MY POCKET!
JUST TAKE IT AND GET OUT!

YOU:

Ugh. Nice do business with you. *(BONK)*

■ ■ ■

You drive home with your rebate, plus a nice bonus. And you proudly display it for your wife. While standing next to the dinner table. After taking the phone off the hook.

YOU:

Look! Rebate!

WIFE:

You remember to pick up bread?

YOU:

Bread? No.

WIFE:

(BONK)

YOU:

(aggression display) RAAHHHH!

WIFE:

RAAAHHHHHHHH! *(BONK)*
RAAAAAAAAAAAHHHHHHAHHAH!!! *(BONK)*
RAAAAAAAAAAHHAHAAAAAAAAAAAAAAAAHHHH!!!!!!
(BONK)

YOU:

I go get bread.

WIFE:

First get on table.

YOU:

Uh-oh.

■ ■ ■

3. At the Office

I guess it goes without saying that caveman customs work great at the office. After all, what are office politics, if not brutal and primitive? On the surface we look calm and professional, but deep inside, we know it's jungle warfare. We form warring clans. We lay traps for each other. We even put potted plants on our desks to simulate the primeval forest, and we call employment agents "headhunters."

Come on. Work with me.

How many times have you come up against another employee and lost, not because he was smarter than you, but because on some level, your boss was better able to picture him cutting out a competitor's heart and eating it?

Here are two scenarios to illustrate my point.

Boss:
Come in, guys. I'm about to decide who gets the Larson account.

You:
And what an excellent decision it will be, Tom. I'll bet.

Boss:
Uh, thanks, Stan.

Eugene (your office rival):
I hope while you were thinking it over, you enjoyed those steaks I sent to your house.

Boss:
Actually, it was the strippers that really got my attention.

You:
WHAT?

BOSS:

Stan, I think I'm going to turn this one over to Eugene. Not because he's more competent or even because he has a cool iPhone. But because he's simply more ruthless and less principled than you or anyone else I've ever met. Since I quit working for Amway.

YOU:

Oh, no. This is terrible. What will I tell my wife?

EUGENE:

I'll tell her. I'm meeting her later in the Presidential Suite at the Hyatt.

BOSS:

Meanwhile, there's something you could do for us, Stan.

YOU:

What?

BOSS:

Just to make sure you have no dignity or self-respect left, you could put on a little pink dress and give us a table dance.

EUGENE:

How about one of his wife's negligees? I have one right here. It's a little torn, though.

BOSS:

Not the red one with the little cutouts!

EUGENE:

I'm afraid so.

Boss:

That was my favorite!

■ ■ ■

Don't let yourself go out like that. Here's how a caveman would handle it:

Boss:

Come in, guys. I'm about to decide who gets the Larson account.

You:

Ook ook ook ook ook ook. *(You shamble behind* boss's *chair and start picking through his hair for ticks.)*

Eugene:

I hope while you were thinking it over, you enjoyed those steaks I sent to your house.

"Ook ook ook ook ook ook."

Boss:

Was that what that was? All I found was a pile of mangled meat with footprints and teethmarks on it. *(From behind the* boss, *you show* eugene *your canines.)*

Eugene:

Well . . . gee. I better complain to FedEx about that. What about the strippers?

Boss:

Strippers? What strippers?

Eugene:

The strippers didn't show up?

Boss:

No. Wait. I did find a nurse's uniform in my yard. Looked like someone had torn it apart with his teeth.

You:

(displaying a tick you just pulled) OOK OOK OOK OOK!

Boss:

Dang, Stan. That's a whopper! Put it in my "out" box with the others.

You:

Ook.

Boss:

Anyway, I'm still not a hundred percent sure which one of you should handle the Larson account. On the one hand, Stan works long hours and takes great pride in his work. On the other, Eugene is possibly the most underhanded and conniving little weasel I've ever met. At least since giving Michael Moore a tour of the plant. So I was thinking I'd let each of you tell me, briefly, why I should give the account to you instead of the other guy. You first, Eugene.

EUGENE:

I'll do absolutely anything to succeed, I have no conscience, and I make a good impression because I wear a suit instead of a moldy piece of bearskin.

BOSS:

Stan?

YOU:

RAHHHHHHHHHHHHHHHHHHH!
(You rip off your bearskin, tear an ink cartridge open with your teeth, paint yourself red and yellow, and leap on to the Boss's desk, where you put on a marvelous aggression display, putting Post-it notes in your hair and making suggestive motions at EUGENE *while holding the base of a desk lamp against your groin.)*
RAAHHHHHHH!!!!! RAHHHHH!!!!!! RRAAAAHHHH!!!!
(You finish up by taking a decanter of Scotch from the Boss's sideboard, emptying it on your body while you jump up and down, and using it to beat EUGENE *senseless.)*

BOSS:

He was a slick operator, Stan. But frankly, there is no substitute for team spirit. The account is yours.

YOU:

Oook.

■ ■ ■

Eat Like a Caveman

I've been asked to provide a few examples of caveman cuisine. Unfortunately, Hal didn't give a lot of details. Probably because Susan did most of the cooking. But I can tell you that the cave-food ethic survives in many cultures. You can even find it in our finest restaurants. Have you ever been to Ruth's Chris? They take huge, fatty, slightly decayed hunks of dead cow and they broil the hell out of them with an open flame. Then they serve them with gigantic baked tubers on the side. Close your eyes while you chew, and it's like Barbecue Night down by the old communal fire.

I guess I can give you one example of a cavemanlike dish that is unbelievably good and extremely popular here in Miami. It's called *lechón*, and it's a whole pig, roasted in a hole in the ground or a wooden box called a *caja china*. Believe it or not, I've helped my buddy Val Prieto (babaloublog.com) prepare many of these, and they're fantastic. After serving *lechón* at a party or holiday meal, a mere turkey will be an embarrassment. It's not a dinosaur or a mammoth, I realize, but the idea is the same, and most paleontologists think pigs probably taste better anyway.

Look, pretend it's a stegosaurus. Don't be a nerd; just go with the flow.

You know what? Forget the hole. It's too hard to dig, and the exertion may sober you up, and nobody wants that. Get yourself a *caja china*. You can buy them from a Miami company called, appropriately, La Caja China, at www.lacajachina.com. Get the biggest one you can afford. They ship. If you're good with tools, you can build your own. It's just a box, three or four feet long, lined with stainless steel or galvanized sheetmetal. The top is open, and into it fits a metal tray that holds charcoal. Just above the bottom of the box, there is a sort of steel-mesh rack, on which you set the pig.

Next you will need a pig. Check around at butcher shops and grocery stores and slaughterhouses. Here in Miami, it's very easy to buy a whole pig, but you may have to work a little harder. You want a pig somewhere between 40 and 200 pounds, dressed weight. And you want it scalded and so on, with the hair removed. Ready to go, just like a roaster you buy at the grocery store.

Sometimes pigs stink. That's because they don't castrate them early enough. I can tell you how to get rid of this smell. Brine the pig overnight in a 16:1 solution of chilled water and baking soda. Most people use salt, but salt won't kill the stench. I invented baking soda brine all by myself, so send me a dollar every time you do this.

You might as well go ahead and get the pig flattened for cooking. You want to mash it out so it resembles a doormat. You can go down the inside of the backbone with a hammer and chisel, splitting it so the ribs will spread. Be careful not to go all the way through the pig.

The next day, you and your fellow hominids will want to flavor the pig. You can do whatever you want. Salt. A rub. But the Cuban way is great, so I'll tell you how to do it. Get yourself some *mojo criollo*. This is a mixture of bitter orange juice (*naranja agria*), cilantro or culantro, garlic, salt, cumin, and whatever else you want to put in it. Lime juice, if you want. Fresh is better, and it's not really critical how much of each ingredient you use, but you can buy jugs of prepared *mojo* at www.cubanfoodmarket.com. Badia and Conchita are two popular brands. Strain the particles out of the mojo and inject it into the pig with a giant disposable horse hypo. You need to strain it to keep the gunk from stopping up the needle. Inject as much as you possibly can. You can't overdo it. Try not to inject yourself by accident. A friend of mine did that once. He shared a needle with a dead pig. I hope I never have to say I did that. Imagine explaining that when you donate blood.

You want the heat inside the *caja china* at around 250°F. No higher. You don't need to completely cover the tray with charcoal, and you should push it to the sides. Give the pig at least three hours in the

I'm sorry I don't have any recipes that actually call for dinosaur meat.
Hey, paleontologists claim birds are actually dinosaurs. Why don't you just go to KFC?

upside-down position, then turn it over and cook it another three or four hours right side up. Toward the end, spray the skin with salty water. You want the skin to get cooked and crisp, with little browning.

Take the pig out and hack it up with a cleaver or a giant knife. It's traditional to pass out hunks of crispy skin while you're doing the carving.

(Look, I'm sorry I don't have any recipes that actually call for dinosaur meat. Hey, paleontologists claim birds are actually dinosaurs. Why don't you just go to KFC?)

An idiot can cook this dish and get perfect results. It's extremely impressive.

Tell you what. I'll give you the ideal vegetable to eat with this. It's another Cuban thing, but Cubans have a lot in common with cavemen (as American girls who date them will tell you). Hal hated green vegetables, and so do all my Cuban friends. It's all good.

You're going to cook an item called yuca. It's like a big, starchy potato, only a million times worse.

INGREDIENTS

1½ pounds yuca

2 tablespoons salt

¾ cup *naranja agria*

Your best bet is to buy frozen yuca, because yuca is extremely hard and slippery and dangerous to peel. I recommend wearing a fileting glove when you work with it. Although a severed finger would add a nice meaty flavor. If you're determined to use fresh yuca, here's what you do. Peel the yuca and split it lengthwise. Cut it in chunks maybe 3 inches long. It will have a sort of a woody string running down the middle. If you can get it out, do so. If not, screw it. Yuca is hard and slippery, so if you start getting fancy with the knife, you're going to cut your fingers off.

> *Got my mojo workin' but it just won't work . . . on you*
> *Got my mojo workin' but it just won't work . . . on you*
> *I wanna love you so bad I*
> *Don't know what . . . to do*

Whoops, that was the beer talking.

Put the yuca in a deep skillet around 13 inches across. Add water and ¾ cup *naranja agria* (buyable at cubanfoodmarket.com), until the yuca is covered. Add 2–3 tablespoons salt. Boil the yuca for half an hour. Just simmer it; not a fast boil.

MOJO INGREDIENTS

¼ cup lemon or lime juice

1 ounce naranja agria

1 huge onion, sliced thin

6 large cloves garlic, pressed or mashed

1 tablespoon salt

½ cup olive oil or other grease, i.e., LARD—pretend
it's uintatherium fat

Dump the oil in a saucepan or small skillet. Put on high heat. Dump the onions in. Fry them, tossing and stirring, until they begin to brown a little. Pour in the garlic and salt, and fry for a minute or two. Pour in the juice and *naranja agria* and boil the whole mixture for a couple of minutes.

Okay, take the yuca out and drain it. Put the *mojo* in a bowl or mix it in with the yuca. I like it served on the side.

Amazing. The garlic will make you hallucinate, and the gluey, chewy yuca will make you wonder what you ever saw in potatoes. Very nice.

Generally, people squirt lime juice on yuca when they eat it. I think that's a fine idea.

That's about as close as I can come to actual cave food, without writing an ingredient list that includes the word "dung." I think you'll be very satisfied.

Get Your Caveman Drink On

I know some readers will really, really want to try drinking like a caveman. In my opinion, this is a dangerous mistake. Let me be clear. Your own fermented-fruit concoctions are extremely unlikely to hurt you or kill you. However, they will often contain fermentation by-products that cause hangovers that make death seem somewhat tantalizing.

I'm a home brewer, but all I make is beer. I'm crazy, but not crazy enough to blow the top of my skull off with fusel alcohols and other interesting chemicals that develop when you ferment liquids containing honey. And honey is one of the things you add when you ferment berry juice. Don't ask me why; I'm not an expert. I don't brew with berries or honey because I don't feel the need to poison myself when I drink. I'm perfectly happy with "drunk."

I know you're not listening.

Fine. Here is a recipe for five gallons of melomel, a form of mead which is pretty much what Hal would have drunk had he had better technology. Go ahead and make it. Just remember: I told you so.

You're going to need a fermenter. Home-brew sites such as Morebeer.com can help, or maybe there is a home brewing store in your area. The best basic fermenter is a six-gallon polyethylene bucket with a lid and a doodad called an airlock, to release CO_2 during fermentation so that the bucket doesn't explode and throw goo on the ceiling of your frathouse.

Before you use the bucket and airlock, sanitize—I mean, *have a pledge sanitize*—them thoroughly in an iodophor solution (ask the home brew guys) and let the excess drip out. Sanitize everything that touches the brew before fermentation ends. If you don't, you may grow botulism or algae or smallpox or God knows what else in there instead of yeast. Not that these items won't give you an interesting buzz. For all I know.

INGREDIENTS

1¾ gallons strawberries—should be frozen even if fresh, to break them down for fermenting

⅞ gallon honey

3½ gallons water

1 packet dry Champagne yeast or other wine yeast

This is pretty simple. Mash the berries completely. Boil everything but the yeast in a giant kettle until you think it's sterile. Dump it in the fermenter and put the lid on. Leave a few inches of headroom at the top, even if you have to pour out some of the mixture. When it ferments, it's going to need space. I made the ingredient amounts generous so you could end up with around six gallons in the fermenter. You'll lose some of it when you remove it after fermentation, so in the end, hopefully, you'll have five.

When it gets down to 80°F, add the yeast and put the airlock on. Put clean water or vodka in the airlock.

Fermentation goes faster in things that have been aerated. One way to do this is to sanitize a hand mixer and beat air into your slop before adding the yeast. Give it at least two minutes of serious beating. Real men use oxygen cylinders and airstones.

This stuff may explode in spite of the airlock, because fruit pulp may get driven into the hole. You can avoid this by putting a cork in the top of the fermenter, with a wide sanitized hose jammed into it. The hose takes the gas out. Put the other end in a jug of clean water, so nothing can crawl into it and die in your melomel.

Ferment at 70°F or so for at least three weeks. If you know how to use a hydrometer, try to get the specific gravity down to around 1.000 before straining and drinking this stuff. If you use an autosiphon to move it out of the fermenter, you should be able to leave most of the crap stuck to the bottom.

Other berries, like blueberries or blackberries, will also work.

I strongly recommend Assmanhaussen brand yeast. I don't know if it works. That's beside the point. You should use it because the name contains "Assman."

I don't claim this is the best recipe on earth or even that I've tried it. But it will work (i.e., produce something intoxicating yet survivable), and if you're crazy enough to make it, you're probably not the kind of guy who quibbles about minor flaws in his fermented berry juice anyway. There are tons of resources on the Web for people who make melomel, so all sorts of recipes—including recipes that have won mead-fanatic prizes—are available to you.

By the way, you're supposed to bottle and age this stuff for a while. Again, I don't think you're likely to worry too much about that. And you're supposed to serve it at cellar temperature. Never mind. Who am I kidding?

Be careful about getting too chummy with mead experts because they tend to be terrifying nerds who prance around in medieval costumes waving swords they bought on eBay with their allowance. They're not cool, debonair beer guys like me.

Here's an idea that will leave you with less of a hangover and has the benefit of not taking three weeks. Buy fruit punch mix at Costco and make it with two parts water and one part cheap vodka. Or, you know—*screw* the water.

I know it's not as much fun as mead, but it's quick, and whether you're aware of it or not, research (mine) has shown that women can't tell how strong vodka drinks are. Think of the possibilities. And it's a lot easier to get them to drink it, compared to something you and your idiot friends grew in a bucket.

Whatever you drink, and no matter how much you admire Dr. Drambuie-Mason, do not try to replicate his research by throwing peyote in the punch. Unless, unlike me, you don't mind waking up nude in random locations and having to walk home in a trash bag.

Caveman Decorating Tips

I was going to write a chapter on how you could apply caveman decorating ideas to your home. Then I remembered, most of my readers are men. So they're already doing it.

Think about it. When it comes to interior design, men do exactly what they did a million years ago. They drag random objects indoors and turn them into furniture.

According to Hal, the first couch was a dead bear. How is that any different from pretending a giant cable spool is actually a coffee table? And if you're male, don't even tell me you've never used milk crates for shelves. Or put a TV and stereo in an "entertainment center" made from boards and cinderblocks liberated from a construction site. Men are the reason construction companies build razorwire fences and hang things from cranes over the weekend.

I think probably the worst male decorating practice is furnishing a home with chairs and couches found on garbage heaps. A man will see a couch sitting on the curb next to a pile of Hefty bags swarming with flies and assume that because he can't see anything wrong with it, the person who threw it out must be an idiot. Then he gets it home, and he finds out different. He finds the horrific stains on the undersides of the cushions. Or the smell no amount of Febreze can kill.

So although you are completely content to lie on it with the fan going and the window open, your girlfriend makes you and your buddies cart it outside to the curb. Where another man will see it. And assume you're an idiot.

And so the cycle continues. Thanks to men, some discarded couches have been making the circuit almost since Hal's time. And we will eventually take them with us to the stars. And our girlfriends will force us to dump them on vacant asteroids. Where male aliens will stop and grab them. . . .

You're probably already doing the caveman thing at home. But that still leaves the office. Think of the possibilities.

EUGENE (the slimeball office rival):
Hey, Stan, guess what? I've been decorating my office cubicle. Check it out. First, a framed photo of me next to my Bimmer, shaking hands with Donald Trump. Second, a tasteful and discreet, yet striking selection of exotic orchids. Third, my MBA from Stanford. So what's in your cubicle?

YOU:
Much dung. Many scalps. Skull of guy who used to have your job.

■ ■ ■

Dung and scalps may be extreme, but believe it or not, it's completely possible—in 2007—to decorate your office like a caveman.

For example, how about some nice skins? A quick Googling turns up several firms which will sell you the wrapper from just about any animal you want. And they're not all that expensive.

Check out R&R Traders, at rrtraders.com, for bargains like these:

1. Impala—$75 ($90 lined)

2. Nyala (sort of a stripey goat/deer kind of thing)—$90 ($115 lined)

3. Black-backed jackal (really sporty)—$90 (lined only)

4. Crocodile—$250

5. Deposed African dictator, including syphilis scars and Ray-Ban knockoffs—$40

I'm kidding about the last one. Sadly.

What if dead animals just don't cut it, because all your buddies already have them? No problem. Thanks to the Internet, you can obtain

Maybe you'd like a nice human skull. Think how impressed the other "prairie dogs" will be when they see you eating Cocoa Puffs out of it at your desk.

terrifying, prehistoric-looking animals for next to nothing. Get yourself to Kingsnake.com and check out great classified ads like these:

1. "We have one baby green anaconda left right now. We are asking $150 shipped overnight. Email for pics. Thanks."

2. "Three Foot Male Anaconda—This is a beautiful male. He's feeding on f/t small rats, and really does not like to be touched. He bites. Very pretty non the less. $230"

3. "We just got some new baby alligators in this week. All are eating well on small feeder fish and crickets. Here is a pic of one of them. They are big babies. All about 9-11 inches long and fat. Asking $85.00 each plus shipping. We accept pay pal, credit cards, and money orders!"

4. "Siamese X Saltwater Crocodiles ONLY 2 Left. 5 Availble. 2.5-3'Range. Beautiful specimens that turn yellower as adults. 650.00 each. Thanks."

5. "Baby Nile Monitors. Large amount of beautiful baby nile monitors. All healthy and eating well. Pricing from $20.00 each. Please call for large quantity discount information."

See that? *"Large quantity discount."* Buy five of these babies, and you you can probably stock your cubicle for sixty bucks. Once they reach their full seven-foot length, you can forget about people coming in to root through your files.

Maybe you'd like a nice human skull. Think how impressed the other "prairie dogs" will be when they see you eating Cocoa Puffs out of it at your desk. Well, right now on eBay, three are available. And the lowest current high bid is only $127. If that's too rich for your blood, ten bucks is the "Buy It Now" price for an ulna, which will still get lots of attention. Or you can go to Boneroom.com and pick up a sacrum for $75. Makes a great ashtray. Unless your office is smoke-free. Better check before buying.

Maybe artifacts are your thing. eBay's got 'em. Try this: a bona fide neolithic stone knife, only four dollars! Or you can choose from a variety of more upscale knives at Voyage Botanica Natural History's eBay store.

If a knife just isn't big enough to get you noticed at your next meeting, eBay also has a wide variety of stone axes. The handles are generally missing, but you can make your own. Go with a real branch; nothing ruins the effect like PVC pipe.

You might consider buying a few fossils. Although, if you think about it, that doesn't really make sense. Because if you were really a caveman, fossil creatures wouldn't be fossils yet. Right?

Still, your friends probably aren't sharp enough to realize that, and even if they are, you can always cloud their wits with berry juice. So go check out Paleodirect.com. For the piddling sum of $445, they'll sell you what they claim is your very own tyrannosaurus tooth. A crappy one. They charge a lot more for the really good ones. But how many of your friends have even a crappy one?

Finally, what about weapons? Prehistoric weapons are tough to find, because so far, nerds haven't developed much enthusiasm for reenacting caveman battles. However you can find very similar stuff at Alltribes.com. They sell authentic American Indian weapons. Here's my theory: it's the same stuff, once you scrape off the beads.

You may have trouble getting a bow past the stuffy security people in the lobby of your building. Here's a tip: Bows and spears don't set off metal detectors. So hide them in your golf bag.

Appendix
A Guide to Prehistoric Creatures

My publisher has informed me that, due to the liberalization of the American educational system, a high percentage of readers are too ignorant to understand references to obscure prehistoric animals.

On the up side, they have tons of self-esteem and an encyclopedic knowledge of deviant sexual practices.

In order to help, I am writing this short appendix, describing some of the creatures mentioned in this book.

1. *Homo sapiens.* This is you. Don't read anything into it. "Homo" is just Latin for "man." I won't bother illustrating this one. You probably know what modern, civilized humans look like. Just look in a mirror. Unless you have piercings and wear your filthy jeans so low the crotch is between your ankles. If that's you, go look at a picture of your grandparents.

If you can guess who they are.

2. *Creodont.* You should be glad these things are dead. These were primitive carnivores that resembled David Naughton in the '80s horror film *An American Werewolf in London.* Some

CREODONT   MOORE

were small and harmless and downright tasty. Others weighed as much as a buffalo, or to use my own convenient term, three "Moore units."

3. *Apatosaurus*. This is the same thing as a brontosaurus, but paleontologists changed the name and wrote books and papers about it to convey the misleading impression that they work hard and deserve grants. Actually, a paleontologist screwed up and put the wrong head on an apatosaurus

APATOSAURUS   MOORE

skeleton and called it "brontosaurus," and it took decades for them to figure it out. Shrewd observers noted that in order for an animal that size to feed itself with such a tiny head, its jaws would have to open and close approximately five thousand times a minute, and it would have to eat nothing but Wendy's Triples. Weight: 30 tons or 100 Moore units.

To learn more about the embarrassing brontosaurus/apatosaurus kerfuffle, see Elk, Ann (Miss), *Looks Like My Theory Was Wrong*, Oxbridge Press, 1972 (ISBN 0-740-46384-3).

4. *Homo habilis.* If you're a baggy-pants MTV watcher, you may have more in common with these than with *Homo sapiens*. Not just the aroma, but also the 650-cc brain. Cobbled together from tiny bits of bone, by paleontologists who

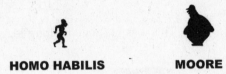

HOMO HABILIS   MOORE

were—again—highly concerned about grant money and the serious risk of having to get real jobs, these little guys supposedly lived in east Africa a couple of million years ago. I think the time frame is way off because, at the moment, one appears to be ruling the nation of Iran.

Bear this in mind. If grant-writers were paying academics to find ancient skunks, the skeletons might look less like Mahmoud Ahmadinejad and more like Pepe le Pew. When it comes to trusting paleontologists, my motto is, "Never forget Piltdown Man."

5. *Tyrannosaurus.* Surely you've heard of this one. It's like a giant hairless kangaroo with tiny arms and eight-inch-long, razor-sharp teeth. And rabies. Extremely vicious. When provoked, it may get so angry it eats its own tail, then stalks away feeling victorious. In the movie *Jurassic Park*, a tyrannosaurus

TYRANNOSAURUS   MOORE ROSIE

ate a lawyer sitting on a dirty public toilet. This was highly misleading. In reality, while a tyrannosaurus would have no qualms about eating a toilet, it would almost certainly be put off by the smell of a lawyer. Weight: 7.4 tons or 24 Moore units plus one "Rosie."

6. *Uintatherium*. This was like a giant, long-legged rhinoceros

UINTATHERIUM   **MOORE**

with ten-inch canines and six big knobs on its head. Weight: about 10 Moore units. A favorite snack of item no. 5, above, the unintatherium was one of the ugliest mammals of all time. On the ugliness scale, most naturalists place it above the Old World sucker-footed bat but just below James Carville.

7. *Wooly Mammoth*. This was like a huge angry elephant in a brown cardigan. It inhabited much of the Northern Hemisphere,

MAMMOTH   **MOORE**   **1 METRIC SEAGAL**

but faded into extinction a few years into the post-Oligocene peanut blight. Differed from modern elephants in that sometimes, it forgot. Weight: 10 tons, 16.7 Moore units, or 30 metric Seagals.

Not all mammoth species were large. There was a species of pygmy mammoth which early man used to capture and train to wash dishes. See Hanna, William D., and Barbera, Joseph R., *Some Day Maybe Fred Will Win the Fight: Appliances and Yard Tools in Stone-Age America*. University of Frantic City Press, 1958 (ISBN 0-250-85741-4).

8. *Velociraptor.* Weight: .05 Moore units or 1.0 Troyers. First discovered in fossil beds in Mongolia, this was a shifty, cunning predator that ran around on its hind legs, looking for

VELOCIRAPTOR   MOORE   TROYER

things to kill. It was surprisingly intelligent for a dinosaur, meaning it rarely forgot to breathe. Sometimes they brought down their own prey, but most of the time, they scavenged in packs, stealing and feeding on items other dinosaurs had already found. Much like modern-day journalists.

Velociraptors were roughly the size of turkeys. I know it may upset you to read that. And I guess it makes Hal look bad, since he was so scared of them. In Hal's defense, he himself was only around three feet, six inches tall. And velociraptors were very feisty. And like Sun Tzu said in *The Art of War*, never underestimate the damage that can be done by a single highly motivated turkey.